ETRUSCAN
Myths

THE · LEGENDARY · PAST

ETRUSCAN
Myths

**LARISSA BONFANTE AND
JUDITH SWADDLING**

Published in co-operation with
BRITISH MUSEUM PRESS
UNIVERSITY OF TEXAS PRESS, AUSTIN

For Giuliano and Vittoria Dompé Bonfante, and Cyril and
Dorothy May Swaddling

The authors are grateful to the following for their help in the
preparation of this book: Irène Aghion, Isabel Andrews, Susan Bird,
Robert Broomfield, Lucilla Burn, Hugo Chapman, G.C. Cianferoni,
Richard De Puma, Helen Dunn, Joan Edwards, Adriana Emiliozzi, Cindy Forrest,
Colin Grant, Nancy de Grummond, M.C. Guidotti, Sybille Haynes, Dudley Hubbard,
Ivor Kerslake, Janet Larkin, Ellen Macnamara, Joan Mertens, Kate Morton,
Tom Rasmussen, Francesca Serra Ridgway, Paul Roberts, Nina Shandloff, Stephan
Steingräber, Thomas Swaddling, Paul Taylor, Alex Truscott, Elizabeth Wahle,
Dyfri Williams, Karoline Zhuber Okrog, and our special thanks to Susan Woodford.

First University of Texas Press edition, 2006
ISBN-10: 0-292-70606-5
ISBN-13: 978-0-292-70606-4
Library of Congress Control Number: 2005034197

Designed by Martin Richards
Cover design by Jim Stanton
Typeset in 10.25 Sabon
Printed and bound in China by C&C Offset Printing Co., Ltd

FRONTISPIECE: *Bronze votive group of man and woman, probably Tinia and Uni
(Greek Zeus and Hera) embracing. In Greek art, too, Zeus and Hera sometimes engage
in stately love-making. In Etruscan art this motif is particularly frequent and emphasizes
the importance of married couples in society. South Etruscan, 500–475 BC.*

OPPOSITE: *Detail from a wall painting in the Tomb of the Bulls, Tarquinia, showing the
ambush of the Trojan prince, Troilus, here shown on horseback, c. 530 BC.*

Contents

What do we know about Etruscan myths? 7

Notes on chronology and pronunciation of Etruscan names 10

The Trojan War 11

The Theban Cycle 21

The Underworld 28

Hercle, Theseus and other heroes 34

Prophecy and the Evil Eye 49

Blood for the Dead 55

The Aftermath 59

The Etruscan Pantheon 71

Concordance of deities 78

Suggestions for further reading 79

Picture credits 79

Index 80

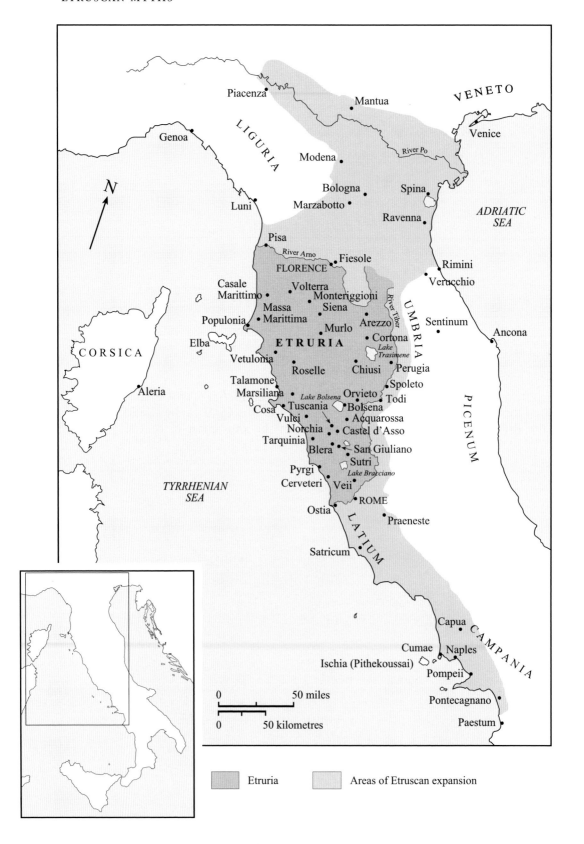

N

VENETO

Piacenza
Mantua
Venice

LIGURIA

Genoa

River Po

Modena

Luni

Bologna
Marzabotto

Spina

Ravenna

ADRIATIC
SEA

Pisa

River Arno

Fiesole

FLORENCE

Rimini
Verucchio

Casale
Marittimo

Volterra
Monteriggioni

Massa
Marittima

Siena

UMBRIA

River Tiber

Sentinum

Populonia

Murlo

Arezzo

Ancona

Elba

ETRURIA

Cortona

Lake
Trasimene

CORSICA

Vetulonia

Roselle

Chiusi

Perugia

Aleria

Talamone

Spoleto

Marsiliana

Lake Bolsena

Orvieto

Cosa

Tuscania

Bolsena

Todi

PICENUM

Vulci

Norchia

Acquarossa

Tarquinia

Castel d'Asso

Blera

San Giuliano

TYRRHENIAN
SEA

Pyrgi

Sutri

Lake Bracciano

Cerveteri

Veii

Ostia

ROME

LATIUM

Praeneste

Satricum

Capua

CAMPANIA

Cumae

Naples

Ischia (Pithekoussai)

Pompeii

0   50 miles

Pontecagnano

0   50 kilometres

Paestum

Etruria

Areas of Etruscan expansion

What do we know about Etruscan myths?

The Etruscans were one of the most important and influential peoples of the classical world. There continues to be much popular mythology about the Etruscans themselves, claiming that they are altogether a mystery, that we do not know their origins and that we cannot decipher their language. These are all misconceptions. There is a great deal that we shall never know about this intriguing people, but what we do know is far more interesting than the so-called mystery. We are learning more and more about many aspects of Etruscan society – their history, economy, social organization and religion – and one of the areas we know best is their mythology.

Before we begin to discuss Etruscan myth, let us put the Etruscans into context. The Etruscan cities which flourished in central Italy between the tenth and the first centuries BC affected the course of history for both the Greeks and the Romans. Their civilization flourished on the west coast of central and northern Italy, with Italy's two main rivers – the Arno and the Tiber – as its boundaries (see map). The Tyrrhenian Sea to the west was named after them by the Greeks, who knew them as Tyrrhenians. The name of the modern region of Tuscany was derived from Tursci or Tusci, the Roman name for this ancient people.

The Etruscans were contemporaries of the ancient Greeks, the peoples of the Near East, Carthage and Rome. Their geographical position in the middle of the Mediterranean put them in the centre of a world in rapid evolution, and their natural resources – great harbours, fertile fields and minerals – made them wealthy. Like the Greeks, the Etruscans were united by sharing a language and a religion. And like the Greeks, they had fiercely independent, highly individual city states, each of which developed specialities in arts and crafts. The southernmost cities on the coast, Cerveteri and Tarquinia, were the first to become wealthy from the international trade they conducted through their harbours in the Orientalizing period. Like most ancient cities, they were located a few miles from the coast for fear of pirates. Their harbour settlements were themselves international centres: Cerveteri's harbour at Pyrgi (meaning 'towers' in Greek) included a Phoenician settlement, while Tarquinia's harbour at Gravisca had an important Greek sanctuary. Populonia, across from the metal-rich island of Elba, was the only Etruscan city to be established directly on the coast: that was because it grew wealthy from metal working, which was carried out directly on the beaches, from where its products were shipped out. Later, between the fourth and first centuries BC, the coastal cities declined, while the cities of the interior – Volsinii (modern Orvieto), Vulci, Chiusi, Volterra, Arezzo, Perugia and Fiesole – experienced a rise to prominence.

The fame of the Etruscans, as the Roman historian Livy said, rang out through nearly all of Italy, from the Alps to the Straits of Sicily. Certainly their artistic influence affected all their neighbours, who in turn became 'Etruscanized.' An Umbrian-speaking city such as Perugia was artistically an Etruscan centre, as was Praeneste in Latium. Rome continued to speak Latin, but was deeply affected by the influence of the art of their neighbours across the Tiber. The Etruscans were in close touch with all the cities of the Mediterranean in the early, international Orientalizing period (eighth to seventh centuries BC). It was then that they adopted both the Greek alphabet to write their own unique language, and Greek mythology, sometimes importing whole sagas and traditions. They also adapted the Greek representations to embody the characters and stories of their own ideology which, for whatever reason, they had previously rarely depicted. Greek vases provided Etruscan artists with one of their richest sources for mythological figures and scenes. Wealthy Etruscan aristocrats imported them in great quantities, used them at family banquets attended by husbands and wives (instead of just single men as was the case in Greece), and after having used them in their houses, took them with them to their graves. Most of the Greek vases which fill the museums of the world come not from Greek territory but from Italy, especially the Etruscan tombs of Vulci, Tarquinia or Orvieto. Greek myths – stories about heroes, heroines and monsters, gods and goddesses in human form – were of great antiquity. For a long time they provided the Greeks with the basis for their prehistory, their religion and their philosophy. When the peoples of the Mediterranean and of Europe adopted them everywhere in the Orientalizing period, they provided a common structure and a prehistory for everyone who formed part of 'classical' civilization.

The richest source of information about Etruscan mythological subjects is their art. The Etruscans decorated their pottery, their bronze furnishings and their chamber tombs with the figures and stories of Greek myth. The artistic evidence consists of hundreds of bronze, stone and terracotta statuettes and architectural sculptures, tomb paintings, coins, carved gemstones, some 3,000 incised bronze mirrors, and similar numbers of decorated funerary ash urns of alabaster, stone, and terracotta, ranging in date from the seventh to the first century BC. Objects made for private use, such as mirrors and gems, are often decorated with figures of divinities, prophets, heroes and heroines, and these characters are often identified by the names inscribed next to them, providing us with, as it were, 'picture bilinguals'.

Etruscans decorated their temples with figures and scenes from mythology, emphasizing the importance of the gods' power over mortals. They used the 'apotropaic' power of images to protect their temples and tombs and drive away evil demons. But unlike the Greeks, who in time discouraged private displays of wealth and power and whose graves have yielded little beyond funerary markers before the Hellenistic period, Etruscans dedicated much of their art to the funerary sphere, to their tombs, sarcophagi, and ash urns. Archaeologists and tomb robbers have in the past concentrated their efforts on the necropoleis or cities of the dead and on recovering the gold and bronze and other precious objects placed in their richly appointed graves.

Like the Egyptians, the Etruscans believed in some kind of afterlife. The chamber tombs from which most Etruscan objects have come were richly furnished because Etruscan aristocrats needed to show their status, and used their conspicuous wealth to demonstrate their culture, good taste and international contacts. But, above all, the richness of their family tombs expressed private devotion to the generations of ancestors that preceded them, the importance of the family and of its continuity in the afterworld as well as in future generations.

From the rich and abundant repertoire of Greek myths the Etruscans chose certain kinds of subjects, often showing them in a special light, emphasizing different characters, imbuing them with a different meaning or adding figures which would have been surprising in the original Greek context. The choice of objects on which they represented these myths was also different from that of the Greeks, and tells us something about their life, religion and society. The importance of women in Etruscan society, for example, is shown by the fact that our richest source for mythological figures and scenes are the bronze mirrors made for women to use in their lifetime and take to their graves for the afterlife. In contrast, Greek mythological scenes occur mostly on the black- and red-figure vases made as symposium or drinking ware for the men of Athens to use at their social drinking parties.

Another source of information is supplied by inscriptions. Objects and inscriptions found at sanctuaries tell us about the gods worshipped and represented by the Etruscans. The most famous are three gold tablets found at the sanctuary at Pyrgi, the harbour of Cerveteri (Caere), in 1964. They are 'bilingual' because they are written in both Etruscan and Phoenician, and they record the dedication of a gift by the king of Caere to Uni/Astarte, that is, the Phoenician Astarte, here identified with the Etruscan goddess Uni. The Etruscans adopted the Greek alphabet into their own language with great enthusiasm, and soon became an extremely literate people. Altogether more than 10,000 inscriptions in the Etruscan language have survived. There were also undoubtedly once Etruscan literary texts, epic poems, drama and local legends. Not one of these, or the books and written texts of prophecies and rituals which were so important in their culture and religion, has survived. Inscriptions, on the other hand, have come down to us as part of the archaeological heritage from Etruscan tombs, cities and sanctuaries. They consist of religious and ritual texts, funerary epitaphs, votive inscriptions and labels identifying mythological figures represented in art. From the religious and ritual texts, and dedications written on gifts to the gods, like the gold tablets from Pyrgi, we learn the names of Etruscan gods. Many of these have been identified with Greek divinities who were more or less close to them in character and function.

The half dozen or so longer texts are religious and ritual, and tell us something about the native gods that the Etruscans actually worshipped. The longest

(2,000 words) is on the Zagreb mummy wrappings, preserved today in the Zagreb Archaeological Museum. It originally belonged to a religious text of the Hellenistic period, a sacred linen book partly preserved by being used to wrap an Egyptian mummy. It names such gods as Nethuns, the Etruscan name for Neptune, to whom offerings of wine were to be made on certain days. The second longest inscription is on the so-called Capua tile in the Berlin Museum, also a religious calendar; it names gods such as Letham, important in ritual but not in mythology.

More important for our subject is the curious religious text on the Piacenza Liver, also of Hellenistic date. This life-size bronze model of a sheep liver, found near Piacenza in northern Italy, was perhaps used by a priest in the Roman army. It was intended for guidance with reading the entrails of sacrificed animals, and is inscribed with the names of twenty-one Etruscan divinities. Some of these can be identified with Greek and Roman gods: *Tin* was equivalent to Zeus or Jupiter; *Uni*, Hera or Juno; *Hercle*, Hercules; *Fufluns*, Dionysos, Bacchus; *Selvans*, Silvanus. Also included are *Usil*, the sun, and *Tiur*, the moon, as well as *Catha*, an Etruscan solar divinity, and *Cel*, a mother goddess. We learn from this and other religious inscriptions that there were many native gods worshipped by the Etruscans who were not those of Greek mythology.

We hope that this book will inspire readers to look for representations of Etruscan myths on Etruscan objects in the British Museum and other museums around the world, and at the Etruscan sites so sensitively described by D.H. Lawrence in *Etruscan Places*, first published in 1932. They can also look for them in the books and articles listed in the further reading at the end of this book.

Note on chronology

In this book we use the conventional chronological terms of Greek art history, adapted to the different situation of Etruscan history.

1. The Iron Age (proto-Etruscan or Villanovan period) tenth to ninth centuries BC (*c.* 1000–800 BC).
2. The Orientalizing period: eighth to seventh centuries BC (*c.* 800–600 BC).
3. The Archaic period: sixth to mid-fifth centuries BC (600–450 BC).
4. The Classical period: fifth and fourth centuries BC (450–300 BC).
5. The Hellenistic period: 300–100 BC.

Note on the pronunciation of Etruscan names

The Etruscans did not have the letters *g, d* and *b*, but only the voiceless stops *k, t* and *p*, so whenever *g, d* and *b* appeared in foreign words – Greek, Latin or Umbrian – they changed them into Etruscan *k, t* and *p*. There are only four vowels in Etruscan: *a, e, i, u*, with *o* being absent. In the transcription of Greek and Latin words into Etruscan it is always written as *u*, so *Acheron* becomes *Achrum*, and *Apollo*, *Aplu*. The masculine singular ending is usually –*e*, as in *Hercle* and *Prumathe*, and the feminine, –*a* or –*i*, as in *Lasa*, *Aritimi*; but the names of gods do not always conform to this rule. Sometimes vowels are dropped out or are replaced by 'weaker' ones, less strongly pronounced: *Menerva* becomes *Menrva*, *Apollo* becomes *Aplu*.

The Trojan War

Did the Trojan War, the most famous event in Greek mythology, really take place? In antiquity the event was certainly believed to be true. There was no clear boundary between history and myth, and for a long time – until at least the fifth century BC – the story provided the Greeks with the basis for their history, religion and philosophy. Early on, these myths were also adopted universally by peoples of the classical world, including the Romans, who traced their origins not only from their local ancestor, Romulus, but also from a hero in Homer's *Iliad*, the Trojan Aeneas.

Homer's *Iliad* deals only with a few weeks in the ten-year long Trojan War. Other poets fleshed out the tale, recounting the events that led to the conflict and those that took place after the incidents described by Homer. All these stories taken together constitute the series of myths that make up the Trojan Cycle, a collection that greatly inspired Greek artists and poets. The Etruscans were familiar with these myths from contact with the Greeks, possibly through their knowledge of Greek literature or story-telling, and certainly by way of the many thousands of Greek vases they imported, used in their houses and took with them to their graves.

Such a vessel was the François Vase, a large black-figured Attic crater or mixing bowl, imported into Chiusi around 550 BC. Its 200 figures, all of them carefully labelled, provided its Etruscan owners with a veritable encyclopedia of Greek mythology, and show us where the Etruscans found their models. The principal subject is the procession of gods on their way to attend the wedding of Peleus and Thetis, the most important social event of Greek mythology. According to the myth, Eris, the goddess of strife and quarrelling had – quite understandably – been excluded, and like the wicked fairy who had not been invited to the party in folk stories, she took her revenge. She threw a golden apple into the midst of the guests. On it was written: 'To the Fairest'. In this way she brought never-ending conflict among the gods, and eventually the mortals whose destinies they governed. All the goddesses at the banquet began to quarrel among themselves as to who deserved the apple, and the title. The three most powerful goddesses, Hera, Athena and Aphrodite, took this as a personal challenge and asked Zeus to choose between them. Zeus quite wisely sidestepped the issue. To decide the matter, he ordered Hermes to take the three goddesses to a handsome young shepherd named Paris on Mount Ida, who would judge who among them deserved the prize. When they appeared before the shepherd, Hera promised to grant Paris great power if he chose her, and Athena promised him wisdom. Aphrodite won outright by promising him Helen, the most beautiful woman in the world, as his wife.

The Judgement of Paris was a popular scene in Etruscan art, appearing on an assemblage of five painted terracotta slabs, the so-called Boccanera plaques in the British Museum (FIG. 1). The plaques with seated sphinxes (see cover) once framed the door of the tomb where they were found. Three remaining plaques from the back of the tomb show two closely related mythological scenes.

FIG. 1: *Etruscan version of the Judgement of Paris. Turms (Hermes) brings the three goddesses, Menerva (Athena), Uni (Hera) and Turan (Aphrodite), to Paris, who will judge the beauty contest. Helen, far right, prepares for her marriage. Painted terracotta plaques from a tomb in the Banditaccia cemetery, Cerveteri, c. 560–550 BC.*

To the left is the Judgement of Paris. Paris is recognizable by his shepherd's hat and carries a branch to suggest the countryside. He greets Hermes, dressed in a spiked, helmet-like hat, three-quarter length white tunic and dark mantle. Hermes, who has come on official business (shown by his herald's staff topped by the figure of a bull), seems to be explaining the rules of the contest to Paris as he brings the three goddesses to him. The group is led by Athena, dressed for the occasion in a red woollen tunic, or *peplos*, and armed only with her spear; she is crowned and carries a wreath. Like the others, she wears pointed boots, the latest Etruscan fashion. Hera and Aphrodite follow her, both carrying branches of poppies, an unusual attribute, and dressed in red woollen mantles worn over white linen dresses, or *chitons*. They both hold up their mantles; but Aphrodite, bringing up the rear, holds up her *chiton* as well, hinting at the conclusion of the story as she flirtatiously shows off her legs and tall red boots.

The right side of the Boccanera plaques shows the outcome of the Judgement of Paris. Aphrodite had promised Paris that he would have Helen in marriage in exchange for his vote, and Helen's figure at the far right balances that of Paris. She adjusts her belt, symbolic of marriage, as her three attendants prepare to perfume and bejewel her with the contents of the alabastron (long perfume vessel) and the cosmetic or jewel box they are carrying. Paris and Helen are here shown in a parallel manner, each one carrying out the ritual that will eventually bring them together as a couple.

The adornment of the bride, the subject of the right-hand side of the Boccanera plaques, is one that frequently appears on Etruscan mirrors, often with Helen as a central figure. Alternatively, the scene sometimes shows Hera or Aphrodite preparing for the Judgement of Paris. On a mirror in the British

FIG.2: *Turan (Aphrodite) with two attendants. The winged Achvizr, left, holds up a mirror for her, the other attendant holds a perfume pin. Below, a satyr reclines on a huge amphora, holding a wine cup in one hand and a thyrsus or artichoke stalk, symbol of Dionysus, Etruscan Fufluns in the other. Scene incised on the back of a bronze mirror, c. 375–325.*

Museum, the goddess at her toilette is Aphrodite, Turan in Etruscan, the goddess of love and beauty who directed the course of Helen's life (FIG.2). She sits on a cushioned stool, is richly dressed in a mantle and *chiton*, and wears earrings, tiara, necklace, bullas (pendant amulets) and snake-bracelets. A winged attendant, Achvizr, stands before her, holding up a mirror into which Turan gazes intently. An attendant on the right uses a perfume dipper to apply perfume to her neck from the alabastron she holds in her hand.

Another colourful, lively rendering of the Judgement of Paris on a so-called Pontic vase of the same date and now in Munich shows the shepherd Paris in the midst of his herd. A humorous, witty tone sets the stage for the approaching group, as Hermes solicitously turns around to give last-minute instructions to the goddesses. Hera, queen of the gods, leads the way, holding out her mantle before her in the gesture characterizing her as the wife of Zeus. Athena follows, and lastly Aphrodite, who again daintily holds up her garment to show off her red shoes.

Stories of the births of the principal mortals involved in this fateful event – Helen, Achilles and Paris – were particularly popular in Greek (or classical) myth. Paris was known in Etruscan as Elcsuntre, which is the equivalent of the name Alexander (but nothing to do with Alexander the Great). Paris was the son of the king and queen of Troy, Priam and Hecuba, at whose birth it was predicted that he would grow up to destroy his own city. For this reason his parents reluctantly handed him over to a shepherd with orders to abandon him far away from the city. In this way he would die of exposure, and they would not be guilty of shedding his blood. He did not in fact die, but grew up to be the extremely handsome shepherd, living on Mount Ida in the Troad, who had to choose between the goddesses. Eventually he went back to Troy, and was recognized by his joyful parents as their son.

Another fateful birth was that of Achilles, the son of Peleus and Thetis. Thetis, a beautiful sea divinity, had been given in marriage to Peleus by Zeus, who had originally lusted after her himself. He had, however, decided to avoid making love to her when he learned of a prophecy that she would bear a son who would be greater than his father. Gods, unlike men, do not want their children to better them. Zeus in particular, having overthrown his own father, did not want to suffer the same fate. He therefore saw to it that a mortal should marry Thetis. Thus, the celebrated wedding of Peleus and Thetis led to the birth of Achilles, the great Greek hero who was fated to die young in the course of the Trojan War.

Greek myth also told of the birth of Helen, whose face launched the thousand Greek ships. Zeus made love to Leda, wife of Tyndareus, in the form of a swan, and Helen was born from the egg that resulted from their union. Leda's other children were the fraternal twins, Castor and Pollux, and Clytemnestra, who eventually married Agamemnon, brother of Menelaos. According to a tradition particular to Athens, the egg of Helen was laid not by Leda, but by the goddess Nemesis, the Fate bringing about retribution, who had intercourse with Zeus in the form of a swan. The fateful egg was then presented to Leda, who raised Helen as her own child.

The theme of the Egg of Helen (FIG.3) was a favourite subject in Italy,

FIG.3: *Turms (Hermes) brings to the prospective parents, Latva (Leda) and Tuntle (Tyndareos), the Egg from which Helen will be born. From the inside of a wine cup, c. 350 BC.*

where it appeared on Etruscan vases and mirrors. Six mirrors and two red-figured vases of the late fourth century illustrate the theme in either of two ways. The first has Hermes (Turms) delivering the egg to Tyndareus (Tuntle), the head of the family, in the presence of Leda (Latva). The other shows the whole family, who have come together to welcome the new arrival: Helen's mother and father, Tuntle and Latva, and her two brothers, Castor and Pollux (Castur, Pultuce). The goddess Aphrodite, or Turan, is present in the role of godmother. The Etruscan focus is on the symbolism of the egg and the family gathering, in contrast to the Greek emphasis on the cult of Nemesis.

At the Judgement of Paris, Aphrodite had won by promising Helen to Paris for his wife. The catch was that he had to fetch her himself. Undeterred by the fact that she was already married to Menelaos and living in Sparta with her husband and daughter Hermione, Paris visited Sparta during Menelaos's absence. While there, he violated the sacred trust of hospitality. Protected by the gods, he seduced Helen and sailed away with her to Troy. This was the cause of the Trojan War.

After Paris took Helen to Troy, the Greek heroes congregated to avenge her husband Menelaos. His brother Agamemnon led the expedition. The huge fleet was assembled and ready to set out from Aulis but, at this crucial point, an angry Artemis sent winds that kept the fleet from sailing. Calchas, the seer, revealed that she demanded to be placated with the sacrifice of Agamemnon's daughter Iphigeneia. The sacrifice was duly carried out. According to one version, the goddess took pity on Iphigeneia and carried her off to the barbarian land of the Taurians, substituting a deer without the knowledge of her father or the others. However the episode ended, an Etruscan mirror of the fourth century illustrates a purely native version of Chalchas (the Etruscan spelling) as a winged figure who is reading the will of the gods from the markings on the liver of a sacrificed animal (FIG.4). Later Etruscan artists were also fond of showing the sacrifice of Iphigeneia among the numerous scenes of sacrifice depicted on urns, wall paintings and other objects (see chapter 7).

Homer's *Iliad* tells of Achilles' quarrel with Agamemnon over the slave-girl

FIG.4: *The winged seer Chalchas, with his left foot on a rock in the proper pose for divination, reads the omens from the liver of a sacrificed animal. Its windpipe and lungs are on the table and a water-jug used during the ritual is on the ground behind. Scene incised on the back of a bronze mirror of c. 400 BC.*

Briseis. Achilles felt that he had been humiliated. He retreated to his tent and spent the time with his dear friend Patroclus, taking no part in the fighting. Things became progressively worse for the Greek side. Finally, Patroclus begged Achilles to join them in battle, or at least to lend him his armour, so that the Trojans would believe Achilles had indeed returned, and the enemy be frightened into retreat. But in the battle that ensued Patroclus was killed by the Trojan hero, Hektor. Achilles celebrated his dead friend with a splendid funeral, including the sacrifice of twelve Trojan prisoners (FIGS 41, 42), an incident shown in Greek art only on a vase from southern Italy. With the new armour given to him by his mother Thetis and made by the god Hephaistos himself, the angry Achilles joined the battle once more, killed Hektor and dishonoured his corpse, dragging it behind his chariot around the walls of Troy. At the end of the *Iliad*, Achilles and Priam join together in mourning for their dead, Achilles for Patroclus and Priam for his son, the great Hektor.

Achilles, with all his temper and tragic destiny, remained the model hero for princes, rulers and leaders. Alexander the Great slept with the *Iliad* under his pillow and paid his respects at the site of Troy when he landed in Asia Minor with his Macedonian army. Portraits of Alexander show him as a young, romantic, charismatic leader after the example of Achilles. In Etruria, too, where the stories of the Trojan War were well known, Achilles represented the model of aristocratic excellence and power.

It is therefore not surprising that an Etruscan aristocrat around 550 BC commissioned a triumphal chariot whose decoration reinterpreted this Greek myth. He took as his model the hero Achilles, and asked a great artist of his time to design the scenes represented on the panels of the so-called Monteleone Chariot. It is named after the place where it was found, in a tomb near modern Spoleto, and today is in the Metropolitan Museum of Art in New York (FIG.5). This precious object would have looked as if it was made of gold and ivory, like the chryselephantine (gold and ivory) statues of the gods, for its brightly polished bronze figures once stood out in relief against a background of ivory plaques. On the front panel of the chariot Thetis is shown handing her son Achilles the golden armour made for him by Hephaistos, god of the forge.

FIG.5: *Drawing of the bronze relief decoration from a magnificent bronze and ivory chariot which once belonged to an Etruscan prince, showing scenes from the life of the hero Achilles. From Monteleone di Spoleto, Umbria, sixth century* BC.

The arming of the Greek hero is the model for the arming of the Etruscan prince, the proud owner of this luxurious vehicle worthy of a divine hero. The bronze figures of the goddess and the hero, mother and son, and the armour she hands him once shone like gold. The story of Achilles continues on the side panels. On the left, the hero fights in hand-to-hand combat over the body of a vanquished adversary. The other side shows him at the end of his life, rising upward in a chariot drawn by a winged horse. This image of the apotheosis of the real-life Etruscan prince riding in the chariot thus mirrors that of the Homeric hero, reinterpreted to illustrate the ideology of the Etruscan prince.

Such near-divine honours were dangerous for the prince, and he needed to be protected. The chariot was embellished with apotropaic images which would provide such protection. Gorgon heads are prominently displayed. The one used as a shield device on the armour that Thetis hands Achilles is particularly frightening, with its red-painted ivory tongue and fangs. A second appears on the shield he uses in his duel on the side panel. The Gorgon head was a ubiquitous, apotropaic image in Etruscan art. It was thought to be effective in frightening off evil influences, and protected the living in their triumphs and glory, as well as the dead in their graves.

Etruscan art represented other scenes from the Trojan War, but with a special slant. There were many prophecies concerning the end of the long war. One of these foretold that the conclusion so longed for by both weary armies would be determined by whether or not the youngest son of Priam, Troilos, died before the age of twenty. This prophecy lay behind a major incident of the

FIG.6: *The ambush of the Trojan prince Troilos: Achle (Achilles), left, armed with a sacrificial knife, lurks behind an elaborate fountain, ready to kill the unarmed youth. Wall painting from the Tomb of the Bulls, Tarquinia, c. 530 BC.*

Trojan War, the ambush and death of Troilos at the hands of Achilles. During a pause in the fighting, the beautiful young Trojan prince came down from the city to get water at the fountain. There Achilles lay in wait and killed him, thus fulfilling the prophecy and determining eventual victory by the Greeks.

An Archaic Etruscan painting in the Tomb of the Bulls at Tarquinia (FIG.6) illustrates the event. An armed Achilles hides behind a fountain with statues of lions on top, the water issuing from their mouths. A naked Troilos, wearing only a bracelet and blue pointed shoes, approaches on horseback. A typically Etruscan detail is the wide-bladed knife in Achilles' hand. This knife was used for ritual sacrifices, indicating that Troilos will soon become a sacrificial victim. The picture thus constitutes an Etruscan translation of the Greek myth. Troilos's nakedness is the typical Greek male nudity appropriate for young gods and heroes, but it is also to be read in an Etruscan context, for the nudity of Troilos is that of an unprotected victim. The nakedness of the beautiful youth is also erotic: according to one story, Achilles fell in love with Troilos. The erotic theme, echoed by two miniature erotic scenes on the wall above the door, is apotropaic, for sex and magic are closely related at all times, and such erotic scenes in a tomb were intended to ward off evil spirits.

Before the war was over, Achilles was killed by an arrow shot by Paris and directed by Apollo to the only vulnerable part of his body: his ankle (or heel). His death was followed by the tragic suicide of his long-time friend, Ajax, who had carried Achilles' corpse back to the Greek camp after his death. Ajax had fully expected to be the recipient of his friend's golden armour, but the Greek army awarded it to Odysseus instead. Ajax was so humiliated that he committed suicide on the beach, falling upon his own sword. Several Greek plays and a number of Etruscan objects illustrate this tragic death, including a mirror now in Boston (FIG.7), a beautiful statuette in Florence and a gemstone in the British Museum. Heracles had once held Ajax in his arms when he was a child, and Ajax was therefore invulnerable wherever he had been covered by Heracles' lionskin. Like Achilles, Ajax was therefore invulnerable except for one spot. When Ajax decided to commit suicide, Athena showed him the one place where he could thrust his sword: under the armpit. Etruscan artists were clearly familiar with this detail and the mirror below indicates that the tragic fate of Ajax, like that of another tragic hero, Amphiaraos, was the will of the gods, probably Athena herself, whom Ajax had offended (FIG.14).

After ten long years the Greeks took Troy at last, but only by treachery. Following the advice of Athena, goddess of strategy, the Greeks built a wooden horse and tricked the Trojans into bringing it inside the gates. Inside the horse were hidden twelve Greek heroes who, having thus entered the city undetected, opened the city gates and let in the Greek forces. Stories of what happened at the fall of Troy were told in the *Iliupersis*, or 'Sack of Troy', and in such tragedies as *The Trojan Women* of Euripides, which described the

FIG.7: *The suicide of Ajax. Athena points out to Ajax his one vulnerable spot, beneath the armpit. The scene thus illustates Aeschylus's lost play on Ajax's suicide. His sword is bent from previous unsuccessful attempts. From the back of an Etruscan bronze mirror, third century* BC.

dreadful suffering, enslavement and death of the members of Priam's family. Neoptolemos, the son of Achilles, who had his father's violent temper but none of his nobility, was the worst villain. In the massacre that occurred he killed and beheaded Priam by the altar of Zeus, hurled Hektor's son Astyanax from the battlements, took Hektor's widow Andromache as his slave and sacrificed Priam's daughter Polyxena at the tomb of Achilles. Cassandra, the prophetess who had warned in vain about the danger of the horse, was dragged away from the statue of Athena and eventually taken by Agamemnon as his concubine, together with him suffering a tragic death on his return home to Argos.

Etruscan artists illustrated a number of scenes from the Sack of Troy. On one Etruscan mirror the making of the Trojan Horse is depicted (FIG.27). In the fourth-century François Tomb in Vulci the Rape of Cassandra is shown: she is naked, and clings to a statue of a goddess. Surprisingly, it is a statue of Aphrodite/Turan, rather than of Athena, as in Greek art. After the destruction of Troy, the surviving Greek heroes returned home. Their further adventures were told in the *Nostoi*, or Returns. Helen went home with her husband Menelaos: she had disarmed him by her beauty when he came upon her with his sword, intending to kill her in revenge (FIG.8). Agamemnon's return home resulted in his death, together with Cassandra, at the hands of his wife Clytemnestra and her lover Aegisthos. The story is that of a family curse, like that of Oedipus, to be discussed in the next chapter.

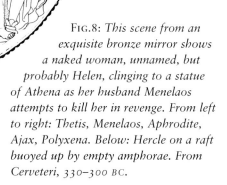

FIG.8: *This scene from an exquisite bronze mirror shows a naked woman, unnamed, but probably Helen, clinging to a statue of Athena as her husband Menelaos attempts to kill her in revenge. From left to right: Thetis, Menelaos, Aphrodite, Ajax, Polyxena. Below: Hercle on a raft buoyed up by empty amphorae. From Cerveteri, 330–300 BC.*

The Theban Cycle

The Theban cycle, a Greek myth tracing a family curse through three generations, was a favourite of Etruscan artists. The story is best known from several Greek tragedies that tell the story of Oedipus, king of Thebes in northern Greece, and of his family. Sophocles's famous play, *Oedipus Tyrannus*, or Oedipus the King, became the definitive account.

Laius, king of Thebes, learned from the Delphic oracle that any son born to him would kill his father and marry his mother. In a moment of lust Laius fathered a child, Oedipus, whom he decided must be left exposed to die. Oedipus was rescued by shepherds and survived to be adopted by the childless king and queen of Corinth, but when he later learned of the prophecy he fled from Corinth to try to avoid his fate, only to fall into a quarrel with a man at a crossroads, whom he killed, not realizing that he was indeed his father. The remainder of the prophecy awaited fulfilment.

In the story to follow, the Sphinx, a terrible monster with a human head and the body of a lion, plays a crucial role. This mythical being was common to the mythology of various ancient cultures, and seems to have originated in Egypt as a kind of guardian of the king. In Greek art and literature the Sphinx was a female demonic being who carried off boys and young men and was present at fatal combats. Like many other monsters, the Sphinx acquired an apotropaic significance and was placed on tombs and other places in need of protection. The monster was very popular among the Etruscans, who also represented it as an apotropaic tomb guardian, often shown as a colourful, beguiling and dramatic figure (see cover).

According to the Theban Cycle, the Sphinx had been sent to Thebes by either Hera or Apollo, depending on the version of the story followed by the playwright. The Sphinx repeatedly asked the Thebans a riddle: 'What walks on four legs in the morning, two legs at noon, and three legs in the evening?' As each of the Thebans failed to solve the puzzle, the Sphinx carried away and devoured them one by one, until Oedipus arrived and solved the riddle. The answer was 'man' for it referred to the three stages of his life. Oedipus was chosen by the grateful populace to be their king, and therefore married the widowed queen. The Sphinx committed suicide or, according to another version of the story, was killed by Oedipus.

Sophocles's play starts with news of a plague that has struck the city of Thebes leaving people and animals sterile: nothing grows or is born. The people ask Oedipus to help them once again, as he did in his youth. During the course of the play, Oedipus learns the terrible truth of the prophecies, and that it was in fact he who was responsible through his outrageous acts for the plague destroying the city he once saved. Horrified at the revelation, he blinds himself and abandons the kingship and the city, attended by his daughter Antigone, who accompanies him into exile. The whole family was cursed by the pollution and died out, for neither of the daughters, Ismene or Antigone, ever married or had children, and the two sons, Eteocles and Polyneices, eventually killed each other (FIG.9).

Following Oedipus's exile it was agreed that his sons would take turns ruling over Thebes. When Eteocles's year was up, however, he refused to hand the throne over to his brother. Polyneices thereupon collected six champions and laid siege to the city. The ensuing battle, the subject of Aeschylus's play, the *Seven against Thebes*, took place as seven champions from each side fought in hand-to-hand combat, one pair at each of the city's seven gates. The play is very visual, as each of the seven champions in turn is described along with his shield device; the Sphinx figures prominently and ominously among these.

FIG.9:
*Polyneices
(Fulnice) and
Eteocles (Evtucle)
fighting over the kingship
of Thebes. From the back
of a bronze mirror,
c. 475–425 BC.*

FIG.10: *In the battles of the* Seven against Thebes, *Tydeus bites into the head of the still living Melanippos, while Athena (left) raises her hand in horror. Terracotta relief from a temple at Pyrgi (Santa Severa), the harbour of Cerveteri, c. 470–460* BC.

Etruscan funerary ash urns of the Hellenistic period often illustrated scenes from the Theban cycle, including the blind Oedipus.

A number of incidents from the *Seven against Thebes* had been popular since much earlier times. The Archaic terracotta decoration of a temple from the sanctuary of Pyrgi illustrates two episodes from the siege. The first is an Etruscan rendition of a Greek myth, the story of Tydeus and Melanippos (FIG.10). According to the Greek version, during the battle at one of the seven gates of Thebes the severed head of Melanippos was brought to the dying Tydeus, who bit into it and gnawed it in bestial fury. The goddess Athena had favoured the hero Tydeus and was bringing him a potion which would give him the gift of immortality. But the sight of this unthinkable deed caused her to turn away from him in horror. The Etruscan artist goes one step beyond the Greek myth in actually illustrating the horror of the deed, showing Tydeus eating the brains out of the head of the still living Melanippos. Behind him the shocked Athena, who was approaching from the left with the little bottle containing the liquor of immortality, holds up her hand to her face in horror. The context of the scene is religious rather than funerary: it decorated a temple, and the appropriately religious moral is to avoid offending the gods.

Another episode from the epic battle on the closely packed sculpture involves the punishment of Capaneus. He scaled the city wall and was fool-hardy enough to send forth a challenge to Zeus himself. The Etruscan Zeus, Tinia, struck down the blasphemous warrior with his lightning bolt. Hellenistic urns show the walls of Thebes and a huge gate ornamented with heads, like the actual gate at Volterra. On one of them a besieging warrior brandishes a severed head as a weapon; on another Capaneus, struck by the bolt of Tinia, falls headlong from the ladder with which he has scaled the wall (FIGS 11, 12, 13). Much later, in AD 1300, Dante's *Inferno* refers to these two scenes as

FIGS 11, 12: (BELOW) *Scenes from cinerary urns from Volterra showing the siege of the* Seven against Thebes. *A warrior uses the severed head of an enemy as a weapon (left). The blasphemous Capaneus falls headlong from the ladder with which he was scaling the city wall, struck by Zeus's lightning (opposite). Both urns were made at Volterra. The arch behind Capaneus recalls the actual arch at Volterra, right, giving the story local significance. Alabaster cinerary urns, third century* BC.

FIG. 13: (OPPOSITE)*The Porta dell'Arco or 'arched gate' of Volterra. The gateway was restored in the first century* BC *incorporating a number of older elements, including heads which may recall the practice of setting up the severed heads of the vanquished as trophies and deterrents to enemies.*

FIG.14: *The Greek heroes, Amphiaraos (the seer) and Ajax, flank a winged figure, who is labelled Lasa but looks more like Vanth. She unrolls a scroll on which are written the Etruscan names of the three figures, Lasa, Aivas and Hamphiare. From the back of a bronze mirror from Vulci, c. 300 BC.*

classical examples of deadly sins: Capaneus shows the height of madness to which sacrilegious pride can bring humankind, while Tydeus and Melanippos become a legendary example of brutal excess and fury. Aeschylus's play ends with Eteocles and Polyneices dying by each other's swords, fighting at one of the gates of Thebes (see p.22). This deadly duel between the two brothers also figured prominently on Etruscan Hellenistic ash urn reliefs. It took place at the last of the seven gates, when the two brothers finally found themselves confronting each other, Polyneices as besieger and Eteocles as defender of the city. After their deaths a herald arrived to announce a decree: while the body of Eteocles was to receive a state funeral, the corpse of Polyneices, who had waged war on his own city, was to lie unburied and unmourned. The aftermath of this terrible siege and fratricide fired Antigone's determination to give both her brothers proper burials, leading to her own eventual death.

That the Etruscans should be so fond of illustrating scenes from the Theban cycle is not surprising. They were evidently familiar with these stories from the Greek tragedies which dealt with them, for although they imported Greek vases in large numbers, the Theban cycle seems seldom to have been represented on them. The Etruscan taste for these episodes is consistent with their pre-occupation with scenes of death, sacrifice, blood and dismemberment, while the moral of the story illustrates the fulfilment of divine prophecies and the necessity of submitting to the will of the gods.

An incised bronze mirror with a purely Etruscan scene shows clearly that these were the connotations in the minds of the Etruscans who commissioned these works, and of the artists and craftsmen who created them (FIG.14). A central, winged female figure unrolls a scroll on which are written, in retro-grade Etruscan script, the words 'Lasa', 'Aivas' (Ajax), 'Hamphiare' (Amphiaraos). These are the names of the three figures on the mirror. Lasa, an Etruscan nymph often shown in scenes celebrating love and beauty, is a winged figure who on this mirror seems to take the place of the Etruscan Vanth, the demon of death. The scroll she holds decrees the fate of the two young men at her side. Typically Etruscan is the importance and solemnity of the written word, which fixes the immutable and pre-ordained will of the gods.

The mirror illustrates a quiet, contemplative scene. The two handsome youths leaning on their shields are shown in thoughtful pose, as if meditating their destiny. Amphiaraos was a seer or diviner who took part in the siege of the *Seven against Thebes*. Because he could foresee the disastrous result of the expedition, he at first refused to join. But his wife was bribed by Polyneices with a necklace, and made him go. Amphiaraos was put in charge of attacking Thebes at one of its seven gates. Like the other six selected champions, he failed in the attempt. He was driven off, and as he fled in his chariot he was swallowed up in a cleft in the ground made by Zeus's thunderbolt. This cavity, it was said, became the famous oracular shrine of Amphiaraos. The dramatic event is shown by the scene in the pediment of the Etruscan temple at Telamon where Amphiaraos looks down into the chasm which is about to swallow him up.

The story of Ajax, one of the heroes of the Trojan War, belongs to a completely different context. The Etruscan artist who designed the mirror has combined the stories of the two heroes in order to illustrate a parallel message he saw in their stories, man's helplessness before the power of the divine will. We have examined the story of Ajax in the preceding chapter and seen how the great disappointment and humiliation of the warrior led him to commit suicide by throwing himself on his sword (FIG.7).

The Underworld

The Trojan War lasted ten years, and the adventures of Odysseus on his way home from Troy took a further ten years. Told at length in Homer's *Odyssey*, and illustrated in a number of the earliest mythological renderings in Greek and Etruscan art, Odysseus's exploits were popular with the early adventurers who, like him, headed for far-off western lands which could easily have been inhabited by the sorts of threatening creatures which Odysseus encountered.

Among the various representations of these stories, one of the most striking is that of Odysseus and the Sirens, with Odysseus shown tied to the mast so he can resist their fatal song. Odysseus also met and outsmarted the beautiful witch Circe (who turned men into pigs), lost many of his men to the man-eating monster Scylla and whirlpool Charybdis, and lived with the beautiful nymph Calypso for seven years before finally returning home to his wife Penelope and his son Telemachos. But Odysseus also had to go down to the Underworld. This was his most famous adventure of all, and a particular favourite of the Etruscans, for whom the journey to the Underworld was an important part of their religious ritual and belief.

One of the most resonant branches of Greek myth in Etruria was the Greek tales of the Underworld. Twice it forms the setting for events in the *Odyssey*: firstly when Odysseus has to visit the House of Hades to learn from the seer, Teiresias, how he is finally to reach his home; and secondly at the end of the book, when the suitors whom Odysseus has killed reach the place of the dead.

These stories remained immensely popular throughout antiquity. A famous large-scale wall painting by Polygnotos, a Greek painter of the fifth century BC, illustrated scenes from the Underworld using material from the eleventh book of Homer's *Odyssey* and other ancient sources. It was called the *Nekyuia*, referring to a magical rite by which ghosts were called up and questioned about the future. This was what Odysseus did when he went down to the edge of Hades, called up the ghost of Teiresias and allowed him to drink the blood of the sheep that he had sacrificed so that the seer would find his voice and tell Odysseus what still lay ahead for him (see FIG. 19). The painting, like Polygnotos's other famous painting showing the *Iliupersis* or 'Sack of Troy', is lost to us. Fortunately Pausanias, who wrote a guide to Greece in the second century AD, included detailed descriptions of both these works. They were well known and often copied, and help to explain connotations and contexts of the images of the Underworld in Etruscan and later Greek art.

The Underworld, as described by Homer, is in fact under ground, the polar opposite of Mount Olympos, which was the residence of the gods of the sky and earth. Odysseus reached it by ship, following explicit sailing instructions from Circe, the witch whose magic Odysseus had tamed. She had fallen in love with him, and only reluctantly helped him to find his way home. After his interview with the ghost of Teiresias, Odysseus speaks with his old companions, Agamemnon and Achilles. He is faced with the stubborn, angry silence of Ajax, still smarting from the humiliation of having been denied Achilles' armour. Then he is somehow allowed to see the far side of the Underworld, beyond the river Styx, which can only be crossed by the dead with the help of the ferryman Charon. He sees famous sinners of mythology who are being punished for their misdeeds, including Tantalos, who reaches in vain for the fruit to quench his eternal hunger, and Sisyphos, who eternally rolls his boulder up a hill.

A remarkable mirror in the British Museum illustrates the Greek story of the punishment of Ixion (FIG.15). He is bound to a winged wheel that rolls everywhere, while he proclaims the need to honour benefactors. His was a terrible sin, for having been welcomed by the gods on Olympos as one of the few mortals to be offered immortality, he became enamoured of Hera and tried to make love to her. Instead he made love to a cloud image created by Zeus, and became the ancestor of the barbaric race of centaurs. The mirror shows the mechanism of the wheel in some detail, according to the practical spirit of the Etruscans.

FIG.15: *Ixion, the great sinner who tried to rape Hera, spinning on a wheel in the heavens. From the back of a bronze mirror, c. 460–450 BC.*

FIG.16: *The nude hero Odysseus (Uthuste) thrusts a huge pole into the single eye of the monstrous naked giant Cyclops (Cuclu). They are identified by inscriptions. Nineteenth-century restoration of a tomb painting, Tomb of Orcus, Tarquinia, fourth century BC.*

The Homeric Underworld inspired the scenes represented in the two-chambered Tomb of Orcus, in Tarquinia, whose name derives from the Latin name for Hades. All the figures in the tomb were once inscribed with their names; not all have survived, but those that can still be seen indicate an impressive array. On the rear wall of the area connecting the two chambers was painted one of the most popular adventures from Homer's *Odyssey*: Odysseus blinding the monstrous, big-bellied, one-eyed Cyclops, Polyphemos (FIG.16). They are labelled with their Etruscan names, Uthuste and Cuclu.

Other inhabitants of the Underworld also populate the chamber tomb. A pensive Theseus was once accompanied by his friend Peirithoos, now no longer visible. Over the hero hovers menacingly the horrible winged demon Tuchulcha, with the beak of a vulture and skin the bluish colour of rotting flesh. Here, as often, Greek gods and heroes mingle with Etruscan demons.

Elsewhere in the tomb, the style is classical, the tone quieter, darker, almost moody. The infernal couple, Hades, wearing a wolfskin cap (chapter heading), and a beautiful snake-haired Persephone, are enthroned as rulers of the Underworld. Before them stands the triple-headed giant Geryon, whose cattle Heracles had brought back to accomplish his tenth Labour. Here Geryon wears Etruscan armour and looks more human than monstrous as he faces the divinities of the Underworld. The banquet of the blessed is still the subject of the paintings decorating the grave of the aristocratic couple who commissioned them, but it has now been transferred to the world below: the table with golden vessels and a servant nearby set the stage for this new location.

FIG.17: *The sarcophagus of the seer Laris Pulenas, who holds a scroll recording in the Etruscan language his family and priestly offices. The relief illustrates the punishment of Sisyphos, shown naked and kneeling (right) with the boulder representing the threshold of the Underworld further to the left. From Tarquinia, third century BC.*

The Underworld played such an important part in Etruscan religion that much of their art refers to its geography, its inhabitants, the arduous journey the dead must make to get to their goal, and the demons who will guide them. In the Archaic period, elite Etruscan families who commissioned artists to decorate their family tombs in Tarquinia chose the delights of the banquets they celebrated in their lifetime and later in the afterlife as their favourite subject. From the fourth century, however, scenes from the Underworld appear with much greater frequency. They take the place of real-life banquets as decoration in funerary art, on the walls of chamber tombs in Tarquinia and elsewhere, on sarcophagi and ash urns, and also on objects of daily life, such as mirrors and vases.

The physical boundaries between the world of the living and the world of the dead held a special meaning for the Etruscans. Artists represented the fortified walls of the Underworld, and the stone that marked the threshold of the Underworld was sometimes, in an imaginative reworking of the Greek myth, shown as the stone of Sisyphos. He was condemned forever to push the boulder up a steep hill, only to have it roll down each time he reached the top.

FIG.18: *The two winged demons, the red-haired Charu, dressed in a short red robe and armed with his hammer, and the bare-breasted Vanth, who holds a torch, stand guard on either side of the doorway leading into a funeral chamber. They are identified by inscriptions. Tomb of the Anina family, Fondo Scataglini, Tarquinia, late fourth century* BC.

Whereas in Greek myth Sisyphos's sin seems to have been his betrayal of Zeus by revealing one of his many love affairs, to the Etruscans his sacrilegious crime consisted of moving this boundary stone from its appointed place: he is shown several times, once in the Tomb of Orcus at Tarquinia with an inscription near his head, *tupi sispes*, 'the crime (or punishment) of Sisyphos'. In the François Tomb of Vulci he appears bearing the huge boulder on his shoulder, and on it perches a winged female demon, perhaps the personification of his crime, guilt

FIG.19: *Hermes Psychopompos (Turms Aitas) leading the ghost of the blind Teiresias (hinthial Terasias), with feminine features and dress, towards the seated Odysseus (Uthuze), who holds a sword. From the back of a bronze mirror, fourth century* BC.

or punishment. On the casket relief of the sarcophagus of Laris Pulenas, on whose lid reclines the image of Laris Pulenas himself (FIG.17), Sisyphos is shown kneeling by a winged Vanth beyond the boulder which marks the outer boundary of the Underworld. He has his hand on a rock, and with a huge effort must seize the boulder that has just rolled down from the top of the height. The Vanth next to him is there to remind him of his guilt and his punishment.

Many scenes feature the two purely Etruscan underworld demons, Vanth and Charu, whose job is not to punish the dead but rather to escort them to their final destination. This is the only aspect of the Etruscan Charu, aside from his name, which connects Charu to the Greek Charon, the boatman of the dead. Vanth and Charu regularly work together as a pair, as in the tomb of the Anina where they guard the door to the tomb (FIG.18). Sometimes two Vanths, rather than Charu and Vanth, flank a funeral scene. They frame scenes of battle, death or sacrifice, thus putting the Greek myths into an Etruscan funerary context. Vanths have been compared to the Germanic Valkyries, present at but not involved in death. There are many of them, and although they all have wings, they have different clothing and carry different items (FIG.53).

Ghosts, too, were important in Etruscan mythology. It is no coincidence that one of the surviving words is *hinthial*, 'ghost', 'shade' or 'image.' In the Tomb of Orcus the ghosts of Teiresias and Agamemnon are each labelled *hinthial* (FIG.45). Not all souls in the Underworld are as heroic in stature as these Greek heroes, however. On the barren tree between Teiresias and Agamemnon tiny souls jump from branch to branch, like the souls of the suitors whom Odysseus kills when he returns to Ithaca. Homer tells how they follow Hermes to Hades like bats squeaking and fluttering in a cave, hanging on to one another and falling off the rock (*Odyssey*, 24, 1–10).

One of the full-size souls is that of the blind Teiresias, the famous Theban seer whom Odysseus went to consult in Hades. His ghost appears on an Etruscan incised mirror identifying him as *hinthial terasias* and representing him as a blind young woman supporting herself on a staff, wearing a man's mantle and woman's shoes (FIG.19). The artist is referring to Teiresias's bisexual experience. According to the Greek myth Teiresias once saw two snakes mating, struck them and was turned into a woman. Later, he saw the same two snakes mating again, and was turned back into a man. When Zeus and Hera had an argument as to whether men or women enjoyed love more, they naturally turned to Teiresias for an answer: he reported that women enjoyed it more than men. Zeus, glad to have won the argument, gave Teiresias the gift of prophecy and a long life, but an angry Hera blinded him. On the mirror, Hermes, labelled 'Turms of Hades', leads him towards Odysseus, who holds the knife with which he has sacrificed the sheep and now guards the blood which the ghosts need in order to have a voice.

Hercle, Theseus and other heroes

Hercle

Heracles was the greatest hero of classical mythology, and the one about whom most stories were told. Such was his popularity that his birth, childhood and adventures were a favourite subject of Greek myths, plays, statues and paintings. He was the son of Zeus by Alkmene, wife of King Amphitryon of Thebes. While Amphitryon was away at war, Zeus had seduced Alkmene by assuming the appearance of her husband, and Heracles' conception took place during a night which Zeus had made longer than usual – the Long Night – so that he could make love to Alkmene for longer. As a result she became pregnant with two boys, each from a different father: the mortal Iphikles, son of her husband Amphitryon, and Heracles, the son of Zeus.

In Etruria Heracles was known as Hercle and, no less than his Greek counterpart Heracles, was hugely popular as the subject of mythological illustrations. He frequently appears on bronze mirrors, as the subject of statues and statuettes and in vase painting, in many of the same scenes that we see in Greek art. In Greek myth it was held that when he died he went to the Underworld but was later taken up to Olympos to reside with the gods. Both in Etruria and Latium (roughly modern Lazio, the area in which Rome was situated) bronze figures of Hercle, Roman Hercules, were dedicated at shrines and sanctuaries, and he became a hero of the Roman army.

Hercle is usually recognized, as in Greek art, by his club and lionskin, which he often wears in imaginative ways designed to cover his nudity. For unlike the Greek hero, normally shown in what is conventionally known as 'heroic nudity', the Etruscan hero/divinity shares the general non-Greek reluctance to appear naked and is often depicted with his loins covered. In the art of Etruria and the cities of Western Greece, Heracles is often associated with fountains and may be linked to a cult of healing springs.

Heracles means 'Glory of Hera', and given Hera's hatred for Heracles, Greek authors had some trouble explaining the name. In fact, in Etruscan art Hera occasionally appears with Heracles in a more affectionate and protective role, as she rarely does in Greek art. Uni, the counterpart of the Greek Hera, wife of Zeus, is often the divinity who protects him, rather than Athena, who regularly stands at his side in Greek art supporting his endeavours. On one mirror an enthroned Zeus – Tinia, the Latin Jove or Jupiter – is shown bringing Uni and

Hercle together and reconciling them, while on a mirror in Florence, Hera/Uni takes centre stage with her adopted son and protégé, Heracles/Hercle (FIG.20). The mirror depicts the symbolic ritual of Uni's adoption of the adult Hercle. In an Italic variant of the Greek myth, Uni (Hera or Juno) is shown suckling Hercle in order to make him immortal. The scene was rarely shown in Greek art, but it appears several times in the art of Etruria, and was clearly important in the religion and myth of ancient Italy. Here Uni nurses at her breast a full-grown, bearded Hercle, whom she adopts in a divine rite of passage so that he will be accepted into Olympos as a god, in the presence of four gods who serve as witnesses. These include Apollo/Apulu on the left, holding a laurel branch; on the right is Zeus/Tinia with his thunderbolt, who points to the tablet which records the divine ceremony and assures its legality. This visual rendering of a

FIG.20: *Uni (Hera/Juno) suckles the full-grown, bearded Hercle, adopting him in the presence of Apollo (Apulu), Zeus (Tinia) and two other gods. Zeus points to a tablet inscribed: 'This image shows how Hercle, the son of Uni, suckled [milk].' From the back of an Etruscan bronze mirror, from Volterra, later fourth century BC.*

document explaining the very ceremony being represented, in which Hercle becomes *unial clan*, or 'son of Uni', is a remarkable example of a 'picture bilingual'. The tablet tells us, 'This image shows how Hercle, the son of Uni, suckled [milk].' The inspiration seems to be Near Eastern, and the scene is similar to that of the Egyptian goddess Isis who nurses Osiris in order to make him a god.

However, more traditionally, Hera was always jealous of her husband's children by other women, and she was particularly hostile towards Heracles and continued to harass him all his life. This hostility was exhibited even before his birth. Zeus had proclaimed that the child about to be born among the descendants of Perseus would rule the land of Argos, so Hera, as goddess of childbirth, hastened the delivery at seven months of Eurystheus, another great-grandson of Perseus and Heracles' cousin, and delayed Alkmene's labours.

A late Greek myth reiterated that when Heracles was a baby, Zeus hoped to get Hera to love him and to adopt him as her own. As it had been ordained that no son of Zeus could come into Olympos unless Hera had nursed him at her breast, Zeus duly tricked Hera into doing so. But Heracles, already endowed with superhuman strength, sucked at it too hard. When the pain caused the goddess to thrust him suddenly from her breast, the milk spurted out into the sky around her and became the Milky Way. Hera continued to stir up trouble for Heracles as he grew up, and even put serpents into the brothers' crib; but, even as a newborn baby, Heracles was so strong that he easily strangled them with his bare hands.

When the boys were grown up, Heracles' cousin Eurystheus, now a king, was encouraged by Hera to order the super-hero to perform many difficult and dangerous tasks. With the sympathetic support of Athena, Heracles succeeded in achieving them all. He was often accompanied by his young nephew Iolaos, who acted as his squire. Twelve of these tasks became the canonical Twelve Labours of Heracles. They are not, however, always the same or in the same order, but include: (1) killing the lion which terrorized the town of Nemea (Heracles is later shown wearing its skin around his shoulders) (FIG.21); (2) killing the Hydra, a nine-headed monster that dwelt at Lerna in Argos; (3) fetching the cattle of the three-bodied monster Geryon; (4) bringing back the wild boar that lived on Mount Erymanthos; (5) clearing the Stymphalian Lake of the flesh-eating birds that infested it;

FIG.21: *Hercle wrestles with the Nemean Lion. Bronze group from an Etruscan incense-burner or candelabrum, sixth century* BC.

(6) capturing the man-eating horses of Diomedes; (7) bringing back the Kerynaean hind, the golden-horned pet of Artemis; (8) capturing the wild bull that was laying waste to Crete; (9) obtaining the belt of Hippolyta, queen of the Amazons (FIG.22); (10) cleaning the dung-laden stables of King Augeas of Elis by diverting a river through them; (11) bringing the three-headed dog, Cerberus, from the Underworld; and finally (12) fetching the golden apples from the garden of the Hesperides, guarded by a dragon at the end of the earth.

FIG.22: *Hercle and Mlacuch, whose name is otherwise unknown; she may be the Amazon queen Hippolyta. This skilled relief composition is from one of the few Etruscan bronze mirrors with cast decoration. The short tang was fitted into a handle of another material. From a rich group of Etruscan grave-goods perhaps found at Adria, near Spina, early fifth century BC.*

Heracles frequently had great adventures on his way to carry out the Labours. The eleventh Labour took him to the Underworld, where he freed Theseus. He and his friend Peirithoos were stuck to the rock on which they had sat when they went down to Hades to abduct Persephone. Heracles unstuck Theseus by pulling him up forcibly, so that some of his skin remained attached to the stone. And that, they say, is why the Athenians were lean-hipped.

On his way to find the apples of the Hesperides, the twelfth Labour, Heracles liberated Prometheus, who had been shackled to the rocky crags at the limits of the world. An eagle daily devoured his liver, but by night the liver regenerated, so that the punishment endured for hundreds of years. A fascinating Etruscan variant of this myth is shown by a bronze mirror now in New York (FIG.23). Hercle has just slain the eagle and freed Prometheus from his bonds, and sits looking on as Prometheus is helped down, supported on either side, in a pose much like Christ being taken down from the cross. Hercle is quite naked, wearing nothing but the strap to the quiver slung on his back, and sits on his lionskin, holding his club. At his feet lies the crumpled mass of the eagle he has shot down with the approval of Zeus. Also looking on is Menrva. Her name, like those of the other characters in the scene, is written above her on the border of the mirror. She holds her hand up to her mouth in amazement, perhaps at the prophecy made by Prometheus (Prumathe) about Hercle and the apples. In Prometheus's weakened state, it is appropriate that the figure to his right should be the doctor, Asklepios, here called in Etruscan, Esplace. Esplace is bandaging Prometheus around his chest, reminding us that the eagle has been eating his liver

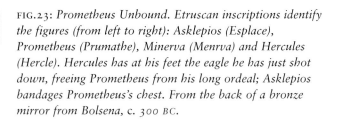

FIG.23: *Prometheus Unbound. Etruscan inscriptions identify the figures (from left to right): Asklepios (Esplace), Prometheus (Prumathe), Minerva (Menrva) and Hercules (Hercle). Hercules has at his feet the eagle he has just shot down, freeing Prometheus from his long ordeal; Asklepios bandages Prometheus's chest. From the back of a bronze mirror from Bolsena, c. 300 BC.*

for thirteen generations. Beside him is a table with more bandages and other necessary medical supplies. The Etruscan artist tells the story with a practical slant, as well as a tongue-in-cheek attitude – there is no equivalent Greek illustration showing Asklepios treating Prometheus after Heracles has freed him.

In return for his slaying the eagle, Prometheus revealed to Heracles that he should not attempt to get the apples from the far-off garden of the Hesperides by himself. This was why Heracles enlisted the help of Atlas, for the Hesperides were the daughters of Hesperis and Atlas and he would know where to find them. Atlas was one of the Titans, a race who had fought against the gods, and the gods punished him by making him bear the weight of the heavens on his shoulders. Heracles therefore went to Atlas and asked him to get the apples while he held up the sky. On his return, however, Atlas refused to give up the apples, so Heracles persuaded him to support the skies for a few moments while he prepared a padded cushion for his head. When Atlas agreed and took back the burden, Heracles grabbed the apples and made off. The story of Heracles' meeting with Atlas, shown holding up the sky on his bent shoulders, was a popular theme in ancient art.

Heracles met a tragic end, for he died by flinging himself on to a funeral pyre, driven mad by the blood of the centaur Nessos. Heracles had killed Nessos for trying to rape his wife Deianeira after carrying her across a stream, but in his dying moments Nessos persuaded Deianeira to keep some of his blood as a love potion to win back her husband's affections, should it ever be necessary. In due course, Deianeira applied the potion to a cloak that she sent to Heracles, but instead of a love potion it turned out to be a poison which drove him insane. Heracles was taken up to Olympos by his patroness, Athena, where he joined the gods, and was given Hebe, the goddess of youth, as his bride. In this, his destiny after death, Heracles was the exception that proved two rules: only the gods are immortal, and even the greatest heroes die.

To end our account of Heracles on a lighter note, several of his adventures are illustrated in comic mode on the so-called Caeretan hydriae, a series of water-jars believed to have been made in the vicinity of Caere, modern Cerveteri. One famous vase in Vienna illustrates a story that takes place in Egypt, where the cruel King Busiris sacrificed all strangers until Heracles' arrival (FIG.24). The Etruscan artist tells the story in the manner of a travelogue, exaggerating and parodying the Egyptian setting. Marooned on a hostile shore, a large naked Heracles, without his usual lionskin and weapons, finds himself surrounded by busy little Egyptians, much like Gulliver among the Lilliputians. According to the law of the land their king, Busiris, must officiate at the sacrifice of the stranger. Here the situation has been reversed. The king himself, distinguished from the rest of the puny white-shirted Egyptians only by the trappings of royalty – a ceremonial beard and a hairstyle like the Egyptian crown – cowers on the steps of the altar. In contrast, Heracles is shown in the manner of the Pharaoh in Egyptian official art, as an enormous figure stepping on his enemies. He destroys four with one blow in the midst of much confusion, turmoil and shrieking. On the other side, dignified Nubian slaves come to the aid of their masters. The Etruscan artist was knowledgeable in both Greek myth and Egyptian art and customs, as well as being very witty.

FIG.24: *A huge, nude Hercules (Hercle) destroys the men of the cruel Egyptian king,*
Busiris, who cowers on the base of the altar. Drawing from a painted hydria, or
water-jar, made at Caere (Cerveteri) in the mid-sixth century BC.

Theseus and other heroes

In Greek art, Theseus was a hero who performed difficult labours, like those of
Heracles. He was especially popular as an Athenian hero, and his adventures
were often depicted on monuments made in Athens. He was often shown with
Ariadne, with the youths and maidens whom the Athenians were forced to send
to feed the Minotaur, or fighting against this bull-headed monster.

The story goes back to Minos, son of Zeus and of Europa, whom Zeus
seduced on the Phoenician coast in the form of a bull, and transported across
the sea to the island of Crete. Minos became king of Crete, and in modern times
his name has been taken to describe the civilization of early Crete. Bulls figure
prominently at various times in the story of his family. His wife Pasiphae fell in
love with a beautiful white bull. Having hired the craftsman and architect,
Daidalos, to build the wooden body of a cow so that she could mate with the
bull and satisfy her lust, she eventually gave birth to the monstrous Minotaur
(FIG.29). She and Minos, who had two daughters, Ariadne and Phaedra, were
ashamed of this unnatural monster, and commissioned Daidalos to build a
labyrinth in which to confine him. Minos also imposed a terrible tribute on the
Athenians, who every year had to send seven youths and seven maidens to
Crete for the Minotaur's delectation – this as a punishment for the Athenians
having killed his son Androgeos. This custom continued for a number of years,
until Theseus, son of the king of Athens, took his place in the group. He

succeeded in destroying the Minotaur with the help of Ariadne, who had fall-
en in love with him. She handed him a ball of wool which allowed him to find
his way back from the centre of the Labyrinth after killing the Minotaur either
bare-handed or with his sword. Having managed to end the ritual sacrifice of
Athenians, he sailed back to Athens from Crete. On the way, he abandoned
Ariadne on the island of Naxos while she slept. The god Dionysos came upon
her, fell in love with her, and when she awoke he took her as his bride. They
remained together as the most affectionate and successful married couple in
Greek mythology, and were often shown together in Etruscan art (FIG.25).
Etruscan artists were familiar with these stories, and represented scenes which
were of particular interest to them. These included the couple Dionysos/Fufluns
and Ariadne, or the god with Semla his mother, Daidalos, the Minotaur, and
Theseus in the Underworld.

The figure of Daidalos was one that Etruscan craftsmen evidently found to
be particularly congenial, for he appears three times on jewellery of the fifth

FIG.25: *Areatha (Ariadne)
embracing Fufluns (Dionysos)
watched by the satyr Syme and
the seated Semla (Semele). From
the back on an Etruscan bronze
mirror from Chiusi. About
350–325 BC.*

41

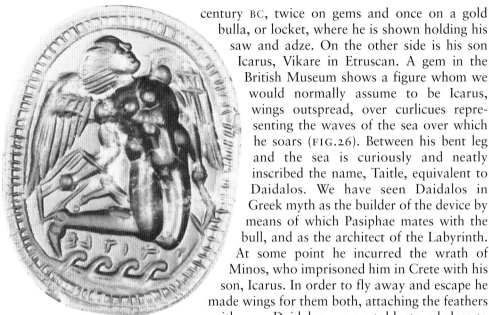

century BC, twice on gems and once on a gold bulla, or locket, where he is shown holding his saw and adze. On the other side is his son Icarus, Vikare in Etruscan. A gem in the British Museum shows a figure whom we would normally assume to be Icarus, wings outspread, over curlicues representing the waves of the sea over which he soars (FIG.26). Between his bent leg and the sea is curiously and neatly inscribed the name, Taitle, equivalent to Daidalos. We have seen Daidalos in Greek myth as the builder of the device by means of which Pasiphae mates with the bull, and as the architect of the Labyrinth. At some point he incurred the wrath of Minos, who imprisoned him in Crete with his son, Icarus. In order to fly away and escape he made wings for them both, attaching the feathers with wax. Daidalos, we are told, stayed close to the surface of the water to keep his wings cool and moist, and this episode in the story may well be what the Etruscan gem carver had in mind when he showed the waves of the sea. The boy Icarus, however, disregarding his father's warning, flew too close to the sun, the wax melted, and he fell into the Icarian Sea, named after him in memory of his tragic flight. Etruscan craftsmen were proud of their skills and practicality

FIG.26: *Taitle (Daidalos) flies over the waves. Demonstrating the Etruscan bent for realism, he carries his tools, and the clamp around his waist shows how his wings were fixed on. Engraved carnelian gem, 450–400 BC.*

and were fond of showing details such as the attachment of the wings. Elsewhere they delighted in picturing details of the construction of the Trojan Horse (FIG.27), and the bandaging of Prometheus's wounds (FIG.23) and of the head of Zeus at the birth of Athena (FIG.28).

Perhaps the most surprising Etruscan representation of the Minotaur shows him not as a fearsome monster, but as a baby in the arms of his mother, Pasiphae, who looks down at him lovingly (FIG.29). In the words of the art historian Otto Brendel, even the monster was once a dear child (*Etruscan Art*, London, 1997, p.344). This is one of the most charming of Etruscan interpretations of the Greek myths, and one befitting their interest in family, children and the affectionate relationship between mother and child; such scenes are not illustrated in Greek art except in situations of terrible, deadly danger.

Two other heroes whose deeds were famous in Greek myth were Perseus and Bellerophon, whose tasks included destroying the Gorgon and the Chimaera respectively. These two monsters that terrified mankind were of special interest in Etruscan art and myth. Perseus was the son of Danae, whom Zeus courted and seduced in the form of golden rain. As a child he was imprisoned in a chest together with his mother, but escaped death. When he grew up he was sent out

FIG.27: (LEFT) *An Etruscan version of the construction of the Trojan Horse. The alert-looking horse, named Pecse, seems to have come alive, as the craftsmen have had to tether his legs while they continue to work on him. Bronze mirror, third century* BC.

FIG.28: Right: *The birth of Athena from the head of Tinia. This is another scene demonstrating the typical Etruscan interest in practical details. Tinia is tended by two 'mid-wives': Thanr, left, who bandages his head, and Ethausva, right, who holds him. From the back of a bronze mirror from Praeneste, c. 450–425* BC.

FIG.29: *Pasiphae nursing the baby Minotaur. From the interior of a wine-cup. Early fourth century* BC.

to behead one of the three fearsome Gorgons, Medusa, the sight of whose face turned men to stone. The Nymphs, guardians of the helmet of Hades which made the wearer invisible, lent him the helmet and fitted him out with winged sandals and a bag to hold the head of the Gorgon after he had decapitated her, while Hermes lent him a magic sickle.

A mirror in the Metropolitan Museum of Art shows Perseus, accompanied by his patron deity Athena (Menerva), with the two Graiai, who kept watch before the cave of the Gorgons and shared one eye and one tooth between them (FIG.30). They are beautifully dressed, as is Perseus, who is shown equipped with Hades' splendid helmet, the curved sickle or *harpe* with which he will behead the Gorgon, and the pouch or *kibisis* in which he will hide her head. According to Greek myth, when he was flying back with his trophy he happened to look down at the sea, and spotted Andromeda who had been chained to a rock, to be sacrificed to a dreadful sea monster. In true heroic fashion he stopped to rescue her, taking out the head of Medusa and turning the monster into a rocky cliff in the sea, and brought Andromeda back with him to be his bride. Stratagems for Perseus to avoid seeing the Gorgon included looking at the reflection in a shiny surface, a mirror or a polished shield. A mirror in the British Museum shows Menerva with Perseus and Hermes at her side, prudently holding up the head of Medusa, viewed in a reflection in a pool

(FIG.31). The head of Medusa became a permanent fixture on the aegis worn by Athena. It was a popular apotropaic device in many aspects of Etruscan art, with examples including temple roofs, the shield of Achilles on the Monteleone Chariot (FIG.5), a gold pendant in the British Museum, and the coins of Populonia.

Bellerophon was the son of Poseidon, who gave him the winged horse Pegasus, born out of Medusa's head when the Gorgon died. The god or Athena also gave him a special bridle with which to catch and tame the winged horse.

FIG.30:
*Perseus,
backed up
by Athena,
confronts the two
Graiai who guard the
cave of the Gorgons. He is
equipped with winged sandals,
a sickle and a bag for the head
of Medusa. On his head is the
magnificent helmet of Hades. From
a bronze mirror from Praeneste
(modern Palestrina), c. 400–350 BC.*

45

FIG.31: *Menerva (Athena) holds up the severed head of Medusa as she, Perseus and Hermes safely view its reflection in a puddle to avoid being turned into stone. From the vicinity of Perugia, Umbria, fourth century* BC.

From the latter's back he did battle with the Chimaera, a female monster with a lion's head and body, a fire-breathing goat's head springing from its back, and a snake for a tail. This deed is illustrated on an Etruscan mirror in New York where Bellerophon flies above the Chimaera on the winged Pegasus (FIG.33). He has already wounded the creature with his spear, and prepares to deal the death blow. The famous large-scale Etruscan bronze statue of the Chimaera from Arezzo might well have once belonged to a similar group including Bellerophon riding on Pegasus battling the Chimaera, shown wounded and snarling up at her opponent, much like the one pictured in the mirror.

Given the importance of women in Etruscan society, the popularity of Atalanta, the athletic Greek heroine who took part in and emerged victorious from the epic hunt for the Calydonian Boar, is perhaps not surprising. The hunt was organized by Meleager to rid the country of a destructive boar sent as a punishment by Artemis. He brought together all the bravest fighters of pre-Trojan War times: Castor and Pollux, Nestor, Theseus and Peirithous, Peleus, Jason, Telamon, Admetus, Amphiaraos, and others. Atalanta drew first blood with a timely arrow, and was given the pelt by Meleager, a fact much resented by his uncles, his mother's brothers. But the hunt ended tragically with the death of Meleager at the hands of his own mother. The Fates had foretold that Meleager would die when a certain log that was burning on the hearth was burned through. Hearing this, Meleager's mother snatched it from the fire and hid it in a chest in order to keep her son alive. When she

FIG.32: *Head of Medusa on an Etruscan silver coin minted at Populonia. The symbols below the head denote its value. About 300–200 BC.*

FIG.33: *Bellerophon, riding on the winged horse Pegasus, thrusts a spear into the lion mouth of the monstrous Chimaera, which has the head of a goat and snaky tail. From the back of an Etruscan bronze mirror from Bolsena, c. 350–300 BC.*

FIG.34: *The beautiful Athrpa, the Greek Fate Atropos, hammers into place a ceremonial nail that affixes the head of the Calydonian Boar to the wall, and metaphorically secures the fates of the pairs of lovers to either side. Scene from a bronze mirror, c. 320 BC.*

learned that Meleager had killed her brothers in a rage, she took the unburned log and threw it back on the fire, killing her son, who felt the burning pain of the fire and died.

Atalanta is often shown on Etruscan mirrors in the company of other heroes, gods and goddesses. She appears on a remarkable mirror featuring Athrpa, the Etruscan equivalent of the Greek Atropos, the Fate who cuts the thread of life spun out by her sister Clotho (FIG.34). Athrpa is about to nail to the wall the head of the Calydonian Boar in the presence of the two pairs of lovers, Atalanta and Meleager (Atlenta, Meliacr), and Aphrodite and Adonis (Turan, Atunis). The picture evidently constitutes a meditation on the story of Atalanta, Meleager and the boar, and the fates that had befallen them all, using the image of the Nail of Fate, an Etruscan concept eventually inherited by the Romans.

Prophecy and the Evil Eye

What was special about Etruscan mythology? First of all, perhaps, the emphasis on female deities, which stands in stark contrast to the male-centred mythology of the Greeks. Few images and symbols are as powerful and universal as those related to sex and marriage, and the distinctions between male and female. It is in these areas that Etruscan renderings of mythological subjects differ most radically from the Greek. In the previous chapters we have noted many examples of the importance of female divinities, of divine couples, of the shifting gender of some minor divinities, and the focus on families, mothers and children. Such peculiarly Etruscan themes, motifs and images, dear to Etruscan artists and their patrons, must reflect something of the Etruscan mentality, and aspects of their own religion and society.

In the realm of religious and ritual scenes, female deities are more important in Etruscan art than in Greek art. The clearest example is Uni (the Roman Juno), counterpart of the Greek Hera. While Greek religion demoted Hera to being little more than Zeus's consort, Uni was a powerful divinity in her own right. Her importance is demonstrated by the famous bilingual inscriptions on gold tablets from the sanctuary of Pyrgi, where she is equated with the Near Eastern and Phoenician Astarte, or Ishtar, goddess of love and war. Another difference between Etruscan Uni and the original Greek Hera is her relationship with Heracles. As discussed earlier, several monuments from central Italy represent Uni nursing Heracles, a subject rarely illustrated in Greek art (FIG.20).

Turan, the Etruscan goddess of love and fertility, is also different from her Greek counterpart, Aphrodite. In Etruscan art we seem to see a juncture of sex and death embodied in the image of the beautiful goddess, not only from a cult statue of Turan found in a sanctuary in the necropolis at Cannicella but also in the inclusion of explicit sexual scenes (in the Tomb of the Bulls) and even pornographic images of sex (in the Tomb of the Whipping) as apotropaic devices, to keep demons away from the tomb. The goddess Turan is represented in a number of scenes together with her retinue (FIG.2). Her circle, often represented on mirrors, includes her young lover, Adonis or Atunis; an Eros or Cupid-like figure who plays with a magic love bird, the *iynx* (woodpecker); numerous Lasas and nymphs; and even Turan's own swan, Tusna (FIG.25). Both the Eros figure and an attendant on a mirror in a private collection are called Turnu, a name that must mean 'related to Turan'. One inscription identifies her as 'Turan ati', and thus a mother goddess.

Unlike Greek religion, Etruscan religion had a number of mother goddesses.

While images of mothers nursing children (the Greeks called them *kourotrophoi*) were rare in Greek art, a woman holding or nursing a child or children appears frequently in Etruscan and Italic art (FIG.35). Even Menrva (Athena) was shown as a kourotrophos, with children. We have seen the charming picture of the baby Minotaur in the arms of his mother, Pasiphae, on a red-figure vase (FIG.29). On an Etruscan mirror in the Museo di Villa Giulia in Rome Helen is shown snuggled up in bed with her daughter Hermione, who is nursing at her breast as Paris looks on.

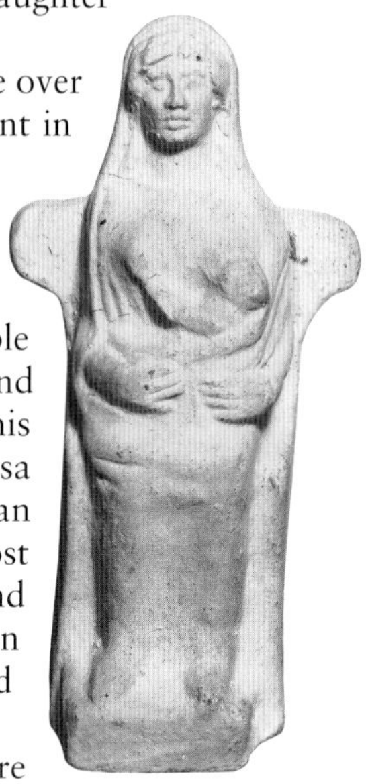

The birth scenes of Greek art, in which the male gods take over the act of procreation from the female goddesses, are present in Etruscan art as well. Athena (Menrva) emerges from the head of Zeus (Tinia) (FIG.28); Dionysos (Fufluns) is born from his thigh and Helen's family welcomes the egg from which she was to be born (FIG.3).

Most surprising of all, perhaps, is the lack of a stable iconography for a number of divinities. Genders, ages and relationships are fluid. Tinia can be a youthful god, unlike his mature Greek counterpart. Minor divinities (Thalna, Lasa Sitmica and Achvizr) associated with the circle of Turan can change gender, appearing as female or male figures. The ghost (*hinthial*) of Teiresias, the blind seer of Greek tragedy and mythology, who had known what it meant to be both man and woman, is represented on a mirror with frontal face and female features, dressed in women's clothes (FIG.19).

Gods appear as couples of male and female figures, more

FIG.35: (ABOVE) *Terracotta figure of a nursing mother, a popular subject in Etruscan art. Such votive figures were often dedicated at sanctuaries, in prayer or thanksgiving.* 450–400 BC.

FIG.36: (LEFT) *Satyr and smiling maenad, from a hydria or water-jar, made at Cerveteri, sixth century* BC.

often than in Greek mythology and Greek art, where only Dionysos and Ariadne are frequently shown as a happily married divine pair. Etruscan art is populated by such couples as Fufluns and Areatha (FIG.25), Aita and Phersipnai (rulers of the Underworld), and Turan and Atunis (FIG.37). Satyrs and maenads, frequently shown dancing together, are on much friendlier terms than in Greek art (FIG.36), where lustful satyrs pursue frightened maenads and nymphs. The pairs are not always married couples or lovers. They can be brother and sister, as in the case of Apollo and Artemis, often shown together in Greek art, or mother and son, such as Semla and Fufluns tenderly embracing. Sometimes gods work together, as partners, like Vanth and Charu (FIG.18). Frequently pairs of divinities are made up of a younger male and an older – and larger – female figure: Turan with Atunis (FIG.25), or a youthful Fufluns with his mother.

This Etruscan emphasis on couples, both divine and human, constitutes one of the chief differences between the Greek and the Etruscan situation in

FIG.37: *Turan and Atunis (Aphrodite and Adonis) with Turan's winged attendant, Zipna, and, left, her swan, Tusna. Around them are more attendants of Turan and, below, a chubby satyr. The motif of a mature woman with a younger lover is typically Etruscan. Fourth century* BC.

mythology and presumably in society. The married couple is ubiquitous in Etruscan art. It is appropriate to the social situation of the Etruscan aristocracy, in which the wife's family played as important a role in the family's genealogy as that of the husband. The social basis of Etruscan society was the private world of the aristocratic couple, in contrast to the world of the male citizen of the democratic Athenian society reflected in classical Greek art, or the *pater familias* of the oligarchic Roman society.

The position of women in Etruscan society was, even in antiquity, the subject of some discussion, as a custom that ran counter to the situation in classical Athens. In a passage devoted to the Etruscans, a fourth-century Greek historian, Theopompus, relates a number of customs which he viewed as notable with regard to the women. His account is in large part a literary cliché about the lustful, luxurious way of the barbarians, but some details are accurate enough to be based on eyewitness accounts of Greek travellers. Etruscan women dine in public, he says, with men other than their husbands – whereas in Athens women actually lived in a separate part of the house. They raised all of the children that were born – no doubt because they were wealthy enough to afford them, and perhaps also because the women could transmit their own status to the children.

Early Etruscan art represented marriage by means of a particularly powerful image, for which archaeologists have a polite name: they call it *symplegma*, or sexual embrace. Such explicitly erotic scenes had the power to ward off evil, and for this reason were sometimes represented in tomb painting. A notable example occurs on a seventh-century vase from Tragliatella, near Cerveteri. They show a man and a woman having intercourse, indicating the consummation of marriage. Where both man and woman are shown embracing nude, such as on 'the sarcophagus of the married couple' in Boston, we can almost certainly assume that the two are married, as we can with the similar sarcophagus in the Museo di Villa Giulia in Rome, where the man's mantle covers the legs of the woman. Two mirrors showing Tinia about to make love to Semla, who is raising her skirt, indicate the conception of Dionysus: they are not married, but it is a sacred union.

Local myths

A basic tenet of Etruscan religion was a belief in divination and the interpretation of natural phenomena as omens, and the many scenes of prophecy in Etruscan art reflect its importance in their religion. We have already seen the transformation of the Greek seer Calchas into the Etruscan priest Chalchas, reading the liver of the sacrificial animal, and of the Fate Atropos, the beautiful Athrpa, on another mirror (FIGS 4, 34).

Occasionally, Etruscan art depicts a historical or semi-historical event. In contemporary Greek art this was extremely rare. A third-century mirror depicts a local myth or legend and records names familiar from Roman historical tradition (FIG.38). In the centre, an Apollo-like youth called Cacu plays a lyre. A boy, Artile, sits beside him listening intently and looks down at an open diptych on his knees, from which he appears to be reading a prophecy. On either side stand armed warriors, half hidden by the trees that frame the seated pair. They are Caile and Avle Vipinas, legendary heroes referred to in Roman historical writings as the Vibenna brothers from Vulci, who came to Rome in the time of the Tarquins, around 500 BC. They also appear elsewhere in Etruscan 'historical' art. A wall painting in the François Tomb in Vulci celebrates the heroic exploit of a group of daring warriors led by Aulus Vibenna, freeing a group which included Caelius Vibenna, his brother. The scene of Cacu, Artile and the Vibenna brothers clearly refers to a local legend involved with Roman historical tradition, one which has nothing to do with Greek myth.

Another native myth, involving an enigmatic scene of a wolf, or wolf-man, in a well, appears on a number of Hellenistic funerary urns and other Etruscan monuments. In the absence of any reference to it in literature, we can only guess as to the stories behind the images. The wolf-skin cap of Hades, god of the Underworld (FIG.49, chapter headings), and the many images of wolves, show that this animal had a special place in the Etruscan mythological repertoire. The significance of the wolf in Etruscan myth is of course attested by the famous Etruscan she-wolf, which was identified with the wolf that nursed Romulus and Remus as babies and became the symbol of Rome (FIG.39). The she-wolf joins other apotropaic symbols, the Gorgon head (FIG.32), the Sphinx (COVER), and many female animals and beings whose powerful magic protected the homes of the gods and the tombs of the dead, and whose female gender evidently rendered them more effective.

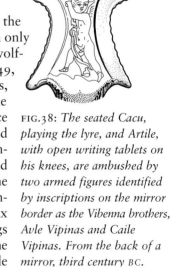

FIG.38: *The seated Cacu, playing the lyre, and Artile, with open writing tablets on his knees, are ambushed by two armed figures identified by inscriptions on the mirror border as the Vibenna brothers, Avle Vipinas and Caile Vipinas. From the back of a mirror, third century BC.*

Apotropaic images

A number of images seem to have functioned, as in many Mediterranean countries, to ward off the Evil Eye and evil spirits. This was the case for the image of Acheloos, the horn-headed river god so often used as a good-luck charm (FIG.40), the head of Medusa (FIG.32), erotic depictions, and even the many scenes of bloody battle and sacrifice. Satyrs and maenads, separately or dancing together, were frequently used as temple decorations, where they served as

FIG.39: *Etruscan bronze statue of a nursing she-wolf, the so-called Capitoline Wolf. The twins, representing Romulus and Remus, were added in the Renaissance (see p.65). Fifth century* BC.

FIG.40: *Gold pendant in the form of a satyr, or the river god Acheloos, usually depicted with his characteristic horns. Both were believed to ward off evil spirits. Sixth century* BC.

protective images (FIG.36). Other apotropaic images involved the sign of the horn, frontal faces and a number of symbols related to Dionysos.

The study of Greek and Etruscan iconography reveals a differing view of the symbolism of gender. The Etruscans used a remarkably wide range of sexual images and often changed Greek representations in surprising ways to express their own customs and ideas. A variety of explanations can help to account for their particular uses of gender and of sexually charged figures, symbols and scenes. Their art shows the connection between sex and death found in so many ancient and modern societies. The emphasis on elite married couples, so clearly a crucial motif in Etruscan art, denoted the importance of the family in this aristocratic world, and the unbreakable thread of familial continuity stretching between generations and between life and death. Etruscan art made use of the powerful force of sexual symbols and images for religious, ritual and apotropaic purposes, to ensure and celebrate the fertility and survival of the family and the lineage, to help the dead reach the other side, to pay homage to their divinities and to protect both the dead and the living. The shock effect of certain images in an unexpected context could serve to ward off evil and fear, and fulfilled a specific 'ritual' or psychological function in the context of religious and funerary art, especially in their tombs, where mortals come face to face with divinity, and the living with the dead.

Blood for the Dead

Scenes of cruelty, violence and death

We have seen that Etruscan artists put a special slant on Greek myths by their choice of stories as well as by the way they represented them. An example of the manner in which their preferences reflected their customs and beliefs is the prevalence of cruel and bloody scenes in Etruscan funerary art. Many Greek myths chosen by later Etruscan artists deal with battles, violence, sacrifice, death and dismemberment. The purpose of such scenes in the context of the tomb was to fulfil a funerary rite, and to provide blood for the dead: the images apparently substituted for actual blood sacrifices carried out in honour of the deceased.

Most striking in Etruscan art is the frequency and variety of the scenes of sacrifice, often differing from those in Greek iconography. We have already mentioned the Etruscan rendering of the mythological scene of the ambush of Troilos (FIG.6). These and other representations show that the theme of sacrifice resonated in the Etruscan belief system from early times.

In the fourth century BC, scenes from the Underworld appear with much greater frequency, taking the place of real life banquets as decoration for the walls of the chamber tombs in Tarquinia. Brutal and violent scenes become more common in other aspects of funerary art, and often show gruesomely realistic details, complete with blood spurting out from wounds. They frequently take place near an altar, and are regularly accompanied by the winged demons Charu and Vanth. It would seem that human sacrifice in Etruscan art took place in a different atmosphere from that of Greek myths, and that it had a background in religious ritual. Here Etruscan ideology differed markedly from the classical tradition of Greece.

Often shown are the sacrifices forming part of the Greek story of the Trojan War: the sacrifices of Iphigeneia, Polyxena and unknown females, the pursuit of Helen, and the rape of Cassandra. A bronze mirror shows Helen seeking asylum from Menelaos at a statue of Athena and depicts her in frontal pose, naked and vulnerable (FIG.8).

The sacrifice of Iphigeneia was a favourite scene in both Greek and Etruscan art. The Greek troops and their allies had assembled under the command of Agamemnon on the shores of Aulis, ready to sail for Troy, to lay siege to the city which harboured Paris and Helen. The fleet was beset by storms and could not sail; then, to appease the gods, Agamemnon allowed his own daughter to be sacrificed at the altar of Artemis. Etruscan funerary urns and later Roman paintings show a pathetic, naked Iphigeneia being carried to the altar as her father stands by, his head covered to denote grief and shame.

This terrible deed was in fact abhorred by the gods, and was avenged by Agamemnon's wife Clytemnestra at the end of the war, when the victorious king came home from Troy and she murdered him, along with Cassandra, whom he had brought home as his concubine. Agamemnon's son, Orestes, eventually succeeded in avenging his father's death, but he did so by committing the crime of matricide, and the Furies, female demons who avenged blood guilt, pursued him to the far corners of the earth. Etruscan artists often showed Orestes with the Furies, whom they identified with their own death demon, Vanth. The Furies themselves are often dressed like the Etruscan Vanth, wearing high laced boots, short skirts and on their torsos simply crossed straps between bared breasts (FIG.18). On one Etruscan mirror a Fury labelled Nathum, present at the matricide, holds snakes, like the beautiful bronze statuette of the demon (FIG.53).

Another scene taken from the cycle of the *Oresteia* by Etruscan workshops deals directly with human sacrifice. In an attempt to escape the Furies, Orestes had to flee to the far-off, barbarian land of the Taurians. Landing in Tauris with his faithful friend Pylades, he soon discovered that, as Greeks, they were both to be sacrificed, and that the priestess who was to prepare them for the bloody ritual was none other than Orestes' long-lost sister Iphigeneia, whom Artemis had miraculously saved from being sacrificed herself. The altar included in this and other scenes indicates the sacred context of the macabre rite.

The sacrifice of the Trojan prisoners, a scene taking up only two lines in the *Iliad* (23. 175–6) and never represented in the art of mainland Greece, is important in the art of Italy. It was an appropriate subject for the grave. Achilles is shown killing twelve Trojan prisoners as a funeral offering for his dead friend Patroclus. The hero appears in the *Iliad* as a magnificent barbarian. Devastated by the death of his friend, he reverts to an ancient practice of offering the dead elaborate and costly funerary gifts, including human sacrifice. This was a custom that had been abandoned by his contemporaries, and one that Homer

called an evil, ugly deed. The fullest representation of the scene in Etruscan art occurs in the fourth-century François Tomb of Vulci, where the scene of Achilles slitting the throat of one of the Trojans before the ghost of Patroclus is framed by the Etruscan demons Vanth and Charu. A similar scene appears on a decorated round toilet box or *cista* in the British Museum (FIGS 41, 42). Ajax brings up other prisoners, naked, with their legs cut and bleeding to prevent them from running away. Achilles' sacrifice of the Trojan prisoners, a purely Italic artistic motif, occurs on half a dozen monuments from Etruria, Etruscanized Praeneste and southern Italy.

Battles are frequently illustrated in Hellenistic art, in Etruria as in Greece. Some are semi-historical scenes, showing Gauls realistically portrayed with spiky hair, tall and wearing nothing but a belt and a torque. Representations of mythological battles like those of the Greeks and

FIG.41: *The Sacrifice of the Trojan Prisoners. The scene below is incised on the bronze box* (cista) *on the right* (FIG.42). *Before Patroclus's funeral pyre, Achilles (Achle; second on the left) slaughters a seated prisoner, whose blood gushes from his neck. Achilles' companion, Ajax, brings forward three other prisoners, while another prisoner, his hands bound, stands nearby. The fully armed Athena (Menerva) is on the right. From Praeneste, fourth century* BC.

Amazons or the Battle of Gods and Giants tend to focus on particularly gruesome details. We saw, for example, the scene of Tydeus gnawing on the living brain of Melanippos in the course of the siege of the *Seven against Thebes* (FIG.10), and the fratricide of Eteocles and Polyneices, the sons of Oedipus (FIG.9), where artists often show the blood flowing freely from the brothers' wounds.

Such representations are consistent with the Etruscan preference for scenes of brutality. Severed heads, often to be found in scenes of prophecy, also belong in scenes of dismemberment, another favorite Etruscan motif. We have seen that Achilles used the severed head of Troilos as a weapon, and a similar scene occurs on an Etruscan urn (FIG.12). The Greek myth of Actaeon on an Etruscan urn shows him being torn to pieces by his own hunting dogs as a gruesome punishment for having unwittingly looked upon Artemis naked as she bathed.

Our meagre knowledge of Etruscan history, gleaned from Greek and Roman historians, includes two allusions to actual human sacrifices. One occurred in the fourth century, in the course of the fierce struggle between the Etruscan cities and Rome, which had at that time not yet conquered Italy. Some 300 captured Roman soldiers were sacrificed as a public ritual in the forum of Tarquinia (Livy 7.15.9–10). Earlier, after a disastrous sea battle against Greek forces, the citizens of Cerveteri had stoned to death all the prisoners. The pestilence that arose soon after persuaded them to send to the oracle at Delphi, who ordered them to expiate this crime by instituting religious rites, games and horse races. This is a close parallel for one of the Greek accounts of the origin of the Olympic Games, which King Iphitos was said to have instituted in order to avert a plague which was destroying the territory of Elis in the Peloponnese.

Legendary scenes of Etruscan cruelty are also found in classical literature. Virgil tells of King Mezentius, who ruled in Cerveteri 'with arrogant sway and cruel arms . . . He would even link dead bodies with the living, fitting hand to hand and face to face (grim torture!) and, in the oozy slime and poison of that dread embrace, thus slay them by a lingering death'. This same practice was ascribed to Etruscan pirates in a fragment of a speech by Cicero (Virgil, *Aeneid* 8.478–88, with Honoratus' commentary).

Human sacrifice had at one time been pretty much universal. It was given up as uncivilized by the Hebrews, who remembered the story of Isaac, and the Greeks, whose mythology was full of the human sacrifices carried out in earlier times. The Romans followed in the tracks of the Greeks in considering human sacrifice a sign of barbarism, and repeatedly attempted to eradicate the practice among the Gauls. But they too had tried it once, in the dark days of the war against Hannibal (Livy 22.57), perhaps thinking that if it worked for the Carthaginians, they too could appease the angry gods in this way.

The Aftermath

The Etruscans in Roman mythology

Roman myth was more consciously historical and religious than Greek myth. As Jane Gardner has commented, 'most Roman myths are presented by ancient writers not as fiction, but as the early history of the Roman people' (*Roman Myths*, London, 1993). The authors who constitute our principal sources for Roman myths, Livy, Virgil and Dionysius of Halicarnassus, wrote at the time of the first emperor, Augustus. Questions of the origin and early history of Rome were of great interest at that time, for Augustus had promised a new beginning for the city. Plutarch, a Greek who lived in Roman times, wrote his *Parallel Lives of Greeks and Romans* around AD 100 and dealt with the character and morals of the great men of antiquity. He too was interested in myths concerning the early history of Rome, and his *Lives* included the first two kings of Rome, Romulus and Numa.

All of these authors enshrined aspects of Etruscan myth and Etruscan reality in their accounts of early Rome, adapting, transforming and re-interpreting original Etruscan motifs to agree with local customs, morals and aesthetic taste. In Roman art, Etruscan iconographic motifs often appeared in different contexts, with totally different meanings.

The roster of Roman gods includes some that show Etruscan influence. Many Roman divinities were identified with the Greek gods: Jupiter (also known as Jove), Neptune, Mars and Venus correspond more or less to Zeus, Poseidon, Ares and Aphrodite. Vulcan, the fire god, was equated with Hephaistos. But as in Etruscan religion, female divinities – Juno, Diana and Minerva, identified with Hera, Artemis and Athena – have a wider range of activities than the Greek goddesses. Minerva is quite different from the Greek Athena, and is much closer to the Etruscan Menrva, from whom she derives her name. For the Romans she was one of the chief triad of gods, Jupiter, Juno and Minerva, with a temple on the Capitoline Hill. According to tradition the temple had been built by the Tarquins and dedicated by Rome's last king, Tarquin the Proud, in 510 BC, just before the end of the monarchy. Together with its triad, the Capitoline temple came to symbolize Rome, and was replicated in all the cities of the Empire.

The Roman Venus Genetrix ('Venus the Ancestress'), the mother of Aeneas, was a venerated goddess in Roman mythology, and a far cry from the frivolous Aphrodite of Homer and the love goddess of later Greek myth. She may have been inspired by the Etruscan image of the powerful goddess Turan, often shown fully dressed (FIG.2).

In these myths concerning early Rome, known to us from Augustan artists and authors, Venus's son, the Trojan Aeneas, was considered to be the ancestor of the Romans. The Greek lineage of the heroes of Homer's poems, both Greek and Trojan, was accepted as part of a convenient, universal classification which related the Romans to the rest of the world where Greek culture had been accepted. The Romans felt that no real conflict existed with their own parallel, native Italic myth of Rome's origin, which told of the descent of the Romans from Romulus and Remus, twin sons of Mars and the Vestal Virgin, Rhea Silvia. They were abandoned beside the River Tiber, by order of the king, but were saved and nursed to health by a she-wolf (FIG.39). The Greek and the local Roman myths of the origins of Rome were in time fitted into a consistent chronology, with the twins taking their place as descendants of the original founder, Aeneas.

Aeneas was the hero of the *Aeneid*, Virgil's epic poem, modelled on Homer's *Iliad* and *Odyssey*, which tells of the wanderings and battles Aeneas had to endure before he could fulfil his destiny, to ensure the future foundation of Rome. Virgil also tells the story of one of Aeneas's staunchest opponents, the cruel and tyrannical Mezentius, king of Caere, whose cruelty is graphically illustrated by the kind of death he devised for his enemies (see page 58).

The most curious contrast between Etruscan and Roman myth concerns the character of Cacus. We have seen the local Etruscan myth or legend on a fourth-century mirror showing a long-haired youth called Cacu with a torque around his neck, playing a lyre (FIG.38). His younger companion or assistant, Artile, sits beside him with an open diptych on his lap, reading or recording a prophecy. Artile belongs to the large number of seers, haruspices, prophets and priests illustrated in Etruscan art, including Chalchas, Lasa holding a scroll, Amphiaraos, and Athrpa hammering the nail of Fate (FIGS 4, 14, 34). The Vipinas or Vibenna brothers who appear on the same mirror, Etruscan heroes from Vulci in the sixth century, are known to us from Etruscan artistic monuments and inscriptions; their stories on the Etruscan mirror and wall painting match what is told about them in the Roman historical tradition.

But the story of Cacus in Roman tradition is completely different from that of the Etruscan Cacu. Hercules, Livy tells us, stopped to rest by the Tiber River on his way back from his tenth Labour, driving before him the cattle he took from the three-headed monster Geryon. While he was asleep, a shepherd named Cacus stole the finest of the cattle, dragging them backward by the tail and hiding them in a cave. Seeing only tracks leading away from the cave, Hercules started to leave. When he heard the cattle lowing in the cave he realized he had been tricked, went after Cacus and struck him dead with his club.

In Virgil's *Aeneid*, Cacus is not a human being, but a horrible monster who lives in a huge cavern on the Aventine Hill in Rome. A fire-breathing son of Vulcan and a cannibal, much like the Cyclops in the *Odyssey*, Cacus fled from Hercules and blocked himself in his cave with a huge rock. Hercules finally got the best of him by removing the roof of the cave from the top of the hill. In both Livy's and Virgil's stories, Hercules earns the gratitude of the local people by destroying the monstrous Cacus. Led by the local king, Evander, they instituted an altar, the Ara Maxima, in honour of their saviour, where annual sacrifices and rituals were carried out in his name.

How was the Etruscan seer Cacu transformed into the Roman thief or the monster destroyed by Hercules? Though the reasons for changing this Etruscan myth are not easy to understand, we see that the Romans were using the myth to explain specific rituals. Elsewhere, they used myth to explain the origin of ancient monuments, statues or other features they saw around them in the city.

In Roman stories of the Etruscan monarchy at Rome, the authors also quite consciously emphasized Etruscan customs which contrasted with their own. Stories of the Tarquin dynasty focus on aristocratic couples such as Tarquin and Tanaquil, while the freedom and status of the powerful wives of the Tarquins reflect the importance of Etruscan women. The first Tarquin, Lucius Tarquinius (his name was originally Lucumo, an Etruscan title), came to Rome with his aristocratic Etruscan wife, Tanaquil. She was twice a kingmaker. Skilled in divination, Tanaquil foretold her husband's coming kingship and helped him gain the throne by becoming popular with the people of Rome. Later, as an older queen, she arranged for their son-in-law, Servius Tullius, to inherit the throne.

The arrogant and cruel Tullia, wife of the last king, the tyrant Tarquin, was also a kingmaker. She conspired to gain the throne for her husband (like an early Lady Macbeth), undeterred at the murder of her sister, brother-in-law and even her own father, the elderly King Servius Tullius. She eventually carried out a deed of unspeakable horror in the eyes of the patriarchal Romans, running over the king's corpse in her chariot and spattering its wheels with her own father's blood.

According to the traditional story related by Livy and others, the Etruscan monarchy at Rome came to an end as a result of a contest between two wives who represented contrasting morals, a Roman matron and an Etruscan princess. Officers at leisure in the course of a campaign decided to have a contest of wives, and rode out at night to see what they were doing. They found the chaste Roman matron Lucretia at home, working late into the night, directing her handmaidens at the woolwork which for Greeks and Romans was the sign of the true womanliness and good housekeeping of the good old days. In contrast, the other wife, the Etruscan princess, was out banqueting with other fashionable young aristocrats, male and female, like the handsome couples in Archaic tomb paintings from Tarquinia. The contest was between Etruscan sophisticated luxury and the old-fashioned Roman morality, the *mores maiorum*, to which the Romans attributed their success.

The story of Lucretia further illustrated the lust and luxury, typical of tyrants, which brought the end of the monarchy at Rome. Sextus Tarquinius, son of Tarquin the Proud and one of the officers involved in the wager, was fired with passion at the sight of the chaste and beautiful Lucretia. He went back to her house, was received hospitably and brutally raped her when she rejected his advances. Lucretia called together her relatives, and then committed suicide rather than live on as an example of unchastity for other Roman women. The resulting scandal involving a member of the Tarquin family succeeded in uniting her Roman aristocratic relatives. According to tradition they drove the tyrannical king and his family from Rome, and established the Republic in 509 BC.

The exiled Tarquin sought help from another Etruscan king, Porsenna of Chiusi, who led the Etruscans in an attempt to re-establish Tarquin as king. Porsenna's siege of Rome saw many heroic acts of valour on the part of the Romans, including that of the Roman maiden, Cloelia. Porsenna had taken a number of Roman hostages and kept them in an Etruscan camp across the Tiber, the river that marked the boundary between the Roman and Etruscan territory. Among these was Cloelia. She bravely escaped, along with a group of girls, her fellow hostages, whom she led in swimming across the river, 'among the missiles of the enemy', says Livy, back to their families in Rome. Porsenna could not help admiring this deed, but demanded that she return, since she was a hostage. Both behaved honourably, she by returning and Porsenna by letting her go, and taking back with her half of the hostages. Not to be outdone, the Romans honoured her by setting up a bronze equestrian statue of her in the Roman Forum. The whole story might be an attempt to explain the presence of an ancient statue of a woman on horseback in Rome – perhaps an Etruscan statue of a divinity or an Amazon.

The story of Mucius Scaevola also takes place in the course of Porsenna's siege of Rome. The story explains his name: *scaevus* means 'left-handed' in Greek, the equivalent of the Latin word *sinister*, 'left' or 'unlucky': his name means 'Lefty'. Seeing the desperate situation of his fellow Romans, the young aristocrat Mucius determined that he would assassinate the king, and armed with a dagger, he made his way to the Etruscan camp. There, he saw the king sitting on a platform with his secretary, distributing pay to the soldiers. Because they were dressed alike, Mucius stabbed the wrong man. When the king demanded to know about the plot against him, Mucius bravely put his right hand on the altar fire, to show how little a Roman citizen cared for pain when acting for glory and his country. He also swore that 300 other youths had vowed to carry out the assassination, should he fail in his attempt. According to Livy's version of the story, Porsenna was deeply impressed with his deed. Fearing other assassination attempts, he negotiated with the Romans and raised the siege. An alternative story, less pro-Roman and more plausible, says that the Romans paid him tribute and he left. The detail that the king and the secretary were dressed in the same way could be genuinely Etruscan: Etruscans had a well-justified reputation for wearing beautiful clothes.

The third of these stories told by Livy, that of Horatius at the bridge, is the subject of the rousing epic, *Horatius*, in Macaulay's *Lays of Ancient Rome* (London, 1842):

> Lars Porsena of Clusium
>   By the Nine Gods he swore
> That the great house of Tarquin
>   Should suffer wrong no more.
> By the Nine Gods he swore it,
>   And named a trysting day,

And bade his messengers ride forth,
    East and west and south and north,
        To summon his array.

When Porsenna marched on Rome, a courageous Roman, Horatius Cocles ('One-Eyed'), urged his fellow Romans to cut down the wooden bridge over the Tiber that would allow the enemy army to enter Rome. While they did this, he volunteered to hold the Etruscans off with only two others.

Hew down the bridge, Sir Consul,
    With all the speed ye may;
I, with two more to help me,
    Will hold the foe in play.
In yon strait path a thousand
    May well be stopped by three...

At first the Etruscan enemy laughed at the three Romans, but soon they saw their front line fall before them:

But all Etruria's noblest
    Felt their hearts sink to see
On the earth the bloody corpses,
    In the path the dauntless Three...

As the army advanced, the bridge crashed down, cutting off Horatius's escape:

But with a crash like thunder
    Fell every loosened beam,
And, like a dam, the mighty wreck
    Lay right athwart the stream:
And a long shout of triumph
    Rose from the walls of Rome,
As to the highest turret-tops
    Was splashed the yellow foam.

Alone stood brave Horatius,
    But constant still in mind;
Thrice thirty thousand foes before,
    And the broad flood behind.
'Down with him!' cried false Sextus,
    With a smile on his pale face.
'Now yield thee,' cried Lars Porsena,
    'Now yield thee to our grace!'

Horatius called upon Father Tiber to help him, and jumped in full armour into the river:

'Oh, Tiber! father Tiber!
    To whom the Romans pray,

A Roman's life, a Roman's arms,
    Take thou in charge this day!'
So he spake, and speaking sheathed
    The good sword by his side,
And with his harness on his back,
    Plunged headlong in the tide.

No sound of joy or sorrow
    Was heard from either bank;
But friends and foes in dumb surprise,
With parted lips and straining eyes,
    Stood gazing where he sank;
And when above the surges
    They saw his crest appear,
All Rome sent forth a rapturous cry,
And even the ranks of Tuscany
    Could scarce forbear to cheer.

Horatius had saved Rome, and was rewarded with a statue.

These and other stories, stirringly recounted in Livy's history, inspired artists and poets of later times. Painters from the sixteenth to the nineteenth centuries loved to illustrate the death of Lucretia, Scaevola putting his hand in the fire, and other heroic tales of Roman valour. Schoolchildren learned Macaulay's poem by heart. Earlier generations read with bated breath Shakespeare's *Rape of Lucrece*.

The historical facts underlying these traditional tales are hard to separate from the fictional, mythological framework. Several names are genuinely Etruscan: Tarquin, Tanaquil, Porsenna and Mezentius. Lucumo was a title. The emperor Claudius, in a surviving speech, identified Mastarna (–na is a common ending for Etruscan proper names, like Porsenna) as the Etruscan name or title of Servius Tullius, son of the first Tarquin and Tanaquil. Claudius knew a good deal about Etruscan history: he had studied with Livy, married an Etruscan wife and wrote a book on the Etruscans, unfortunately lost to us.

The survival of Etruscan motifs

As well as stories about Etruscan gods and heroes, certain artistic images found in later art and iconography hark back to Etruscan models. Nursing mothers, mothers with children, couples, winged figures, demons, unusual varieties of nudity, ghosts and scenes of dismemberment and human sacrifice were all characteristic of Etruscan art and iconography, as we have seen in preceding chapters.

The motif of the mother and child, or the nursing mother (FIGS.29,35) occurs in unexpected contexts. On the Ara Pacis of Augustus in Rome, four mythological panels represent symbolic images of Rome: Aeneas about to sacrifice a sow; the shepherd Faustulus discovering the she-wolf nursing Romulus and Remus; the seated, armed goddess Roma; and a seated woman surrounded by animals and plants, symbolizing the prosperity of the earth and holding two infants on her lap. The identity of this seated woman, one of the best preserved of the group, has been much discussed. Suggestions have included Terra Mater, Venus and Pax herself. One of the babies reaches up for her breasts, but he does not touch them. The classical Greek repertoire favoured by Augustus avoided the motif of a baby actually nursing at his mother's breast so frequently represented in Etruscan art and elsewhere in Italy. Classical artists evidently considered the image to be embarrassingly primitive and barbaric. It was appropriate for animals, but not for humans.

The scene with the she-wolf nursing the twins Romulus and Remus centres on the figure of the most famous of Roman symbols, one that is universally recognized and immensely popular down to the present day. But the Capitoline Wolf, which can be still seen on the Capitoline Hill today, is in fact an Archaic bronze Etruscan statue and was originally not a nursing wolf (FIG.39). She is a snarling, powerful, apotropaic animal, like the female lionesses in the painted tombs of Tarquinia, the Chimaera (FIG.33), female sphinxes or other animals or monsters protecting the doorways of tombs or holy places. The twins beneath the Capitoline Wolf were actually an addition during the Renaissance by the sculptor Antonio Pollaiuolo, though there was probably an ancient antecedent, as a similar group was depicted on Roman coins.

Etruscan motifs can be recognized in a number of later images. At Pompeii, the image of the nursing woman makes a surprising appearance as a statuette representing the story of the virtuous Roman matron Pero, who nursed her starving old father at her breast. The scene is reminiscent of the Etruscan mirror showing the full-grown Heracles nursing at the breast of Juno (FIG.20). This became a favourite Hellenistic motif and was later taken over by Baroque artists who delighted in shocking scenes, especially if they had the mark of antiquity.

Pompeian painting and sculpture showed the Roman god Priapus raising the skirt of his garment to reveal his enormous member. Such sexually charged images served an apotropaic function, and were believed to ensure fruitfulness and success in all areas of life. The gesture of raising the skirt to expose the sexual organs was an ancient Near Eastern motif found in Etruscan art. Greek myth had adapted this type of nudity for the figure of Baubo, Demeter's attendant. The story goes that Demeter was inconsolable in her mourning for her daughter Persephone, or Kore, who had been abducted by Hades, the god of the Underworld. As a result, the earth was barren. Nothing grew, and all living creatures were threatened with extinction. Finally, Baubo made the goddess laugh by raising her skirt, and Demeter broke her fast and began to relent. Laughter, indeed, is an immediate, instinctive reaction to the shocking sight of nudity, and is itself apotropaic.

We should not be surprised to recognize Etruscan motifs in Roman art, for the Romans saw Etruscan art all around them. The nude figures of Atalanta and Helen were painted, says Pliny, side by side in a temple in the Latin city of Lanuvium, not far from Rome. The beautiful Helen and the female athlete Atalanta were favourite subjects of Etruscan artists, and the juxtaposition is already known from a mirror of the fourth century BC (FIG.34). It was even said that the emperor Caligula was fired with a passion for these figures, and wanted to move them to his palace, but he was unable to detach them from the wall.

Etruscan myth in the Renaissance

The influence of Etruscan demonology in Christian art was an important element in depictions of Hell in medieval painting and sculpture. Striking figures of Etruscan demons were translated into a Christian context. The devils in Luca Signorelli's painting of *The Damned* (1499–1504) in the cathedral of Orvieto and in Michelangelo's *Last Judgement* (completed 1541) in the Sistine Chapel depend on Etruscan models, and Charun and Tuchulcha inspired numerous denizens of the Christian Hell (FIGS 43, 44). The Etruscan demon Charun served as a model for Giotto's profile of Satan and for that of his Judas in the Arena Chapel in Padua.

As in Etruscan art, beautiful female winged demons were the partners and counterparts of these ugly, hook-nosed male death demons (FIG.18). Many images of angels with wings can be traced back to Etruscan models. The shape of the rainbow-coloured wings of the angels in some Annunciation scenes of medieval and Renaissance art are very close to those of Vanth in the representation of the sacrifice of the Trojan prisoners in the François Tomb of Vulci (FIGS 41, 42), or of the Vanth in the British Museum (FIG.53).

Probably the most direct influence of an Etruscan art work is that found in Dante at the very beginning of his journey to the Inferno in the *Divine Comedy*. Dante saw the Capitoline Wolf when he went to Rome in the Jubilee year of 1300 (FIG.39). He was so struck at the sight of this ancient, menacing apotropaic beast looking down on the Lateran piazza in Rome, where capital

FIG.43: *Detail of a devil from Luca Signorelli's Last Judgement in the cathedral at Orvieto. The motif of the demon biting into the back of the victim's head recalls the scene of Tydeus and Melanippos (p.23). Painted around 1500.*

FIG.44: *The fearful ferryman of the dead, from the* Last Judgement *painted by Michelangelo in the Sistine Chapel (1535–1541). His strange topknot and pointed animal ears recall the figure of Charu from the Tomb of the Anina family at Tarquinia (p.31).*

punishments were carried out, that he vividly reproduced it in his poem. The description of the animals he meets at the very beginning of his journey to the Underworld, when, in the middle of the journey of life, he lost his way and found himself in the dark forest, includes three in particular. They present themselves before him in turn, threatening him and blocking his path: first a panther or leopard, then a lion, and finally the third and the most terrifying, a thin and starving she-wolf:

> ... a she-wolf, that with all hungerings
> Seemed to me laden in her meagreness,
> And many folk has caused to live forlorn!

(Dante, *Inferno* 1, 49–51, Henry Wadsworth Longfellow translation, 1867).

During the course of the Etruscan revival in Renaissance Tuscany there were many artists who adopted Etruscan images of mythological characters. Much has been written on Etruscan influence in Renaissance art, and there is much more to be discovered. Artists visited the 'painted grottoes', as these painted tombs were then called, and found a profusion of classical models, many of them Etruscan. Etruscan mirrors and painted vases, both Greek and Etruscan, were available and deeply respected as models from 'antiquity'. Though not always specifically recognized as Etruscan, they served as models for artistic images in a variety of contexts. The very fact that they were found in the dark, mysterious underground tombs that surrounded the cities on all sides tended to give these objects a numinous quality.

Michelangelo's *Slaves* (c. 1531), sometimes called *Prisoners*, are tied with strips of cloth that look like the bandages pictured on Etruscan souls, for example on the *hinthial* or ghost of Agamemnon in the Tomb of Orcus (FIGS 45, 46). Their bonds strongly suggest that Michelangelo actually meant the statues to represent souls yearning to be free but enslaved by their earthly bodies.

So the rich body of Etruscan mythological imagery, and some of the

FIG.45: (ABOVE) *Scene of the Greek Underworld: the soul of Agamemnon, wearing bandages over the wounds from which he died, and that of the Greek seer Teiresias* (hinthial Teriasals), *with his mantle pulled up over his head. Between them, on the branches of a shrub, are the diminutive souls of lesser mortals, fluttering like bats. Nineteenth-century restored version of a wall painting in the Tomb of Orcus* II, *Tarquinia, fourth century* BC.

FIG.46: (RIGHT) *This statue by Michelangelo (1513–1516), known as the Slave, or Prisoner, is bound with strips of cloth similar to the bandages of Agamemnon, shown above. It seems to have been influenced by the Etruscan tomb painting.*

Etruscans' ideas, lived on in the place where Etruscan culture had flourished, and enriched the art of those who saw the Etruscan monuments that had come out of the dark Etruscan tombs into the light of the modern world.

Conclusion

Etruscan civilization, which flourished alongside that of Greece and later that of Rome, left a substantial legacy to western civilization. The Capitoline Wolf, the fasces or bundle of rods tied round an axe (the symbol adopted by Mussolini) are today immediately recognizable as symbols of Rome and the Roman

Empire. They were originally Etruscan. The beautiful angels with multi-coloured, outspread wings appearing to Mary in Renaissance paintings of the Annunciation scene are originally Etruscan. So too are the terrifying snarling devils of medieval scenes of the Last Judgement, the Mouth of Hell devouring naked souls head first, and the cruel, gory tortures suffered by the sinners in Dante's *Inferno*. All these images ultimately derive from Etruscan myths known to us from Etruscan art, and bring the Etruscans' rich mythology brilliantly before our eyes despite the loss of their literature.

As we have seen, Etruscan mythology is a complex creation that includes the Greek myths represented in Greek artistic and literary tradition, as well as purely native characters, stories and prophecies. Etruscan artists put a special slant on Greek myths through their choice of stories as well as by the way they represented them, often changing Greek images and scenes in surprising ways to express their own customs and ideas. Their works allow us to see the outline of Etruscan religious beliefs, ideas of magic, funerary ritual and social structure.

Etruscans were deeply religious. Much of their art shows scenes of prophecies and oracles, because theirs was a revealed religion. Funerary ritual was important. The many cruel and bloody scenes of battles, sacrifice, death and dismemberment in

FIG.47: *Painted terracotta antefix from an Etruscan building, showing a woman with bared breasts. This action was believed to ward off evil spirits. From Capua, Campania, c. 520–500 BC. Pliny also records the belief that stormy seas could be calmed by a woman uncovering her breasts. In later times, ships' figure heads were often depicted in this way, presumably because of the same belief. The example right (FIG.48) is a figure of Victory imitating a ship's figure head, from Nelson's funeral carriage, made 1805.*

69

funerary art were intended to fulfil a funerary rite, apparently substituting for actual blood sacrifices carried out in honour of the dead. The journey to the Underworld was also important and is frequently represented in the art that has come down to us.

The remarkably wide range of sexual images and symbols can be explained by the fact that sex and magic are closely related at all times. Erotic scenes in a tomb, for example, were thought to be effective in warding off evil spirits. The powerful force of sexual motifs, symbols, images and connotations served religious, ritual and apotropaic purposes. They ensured and celebrated the fertility and survival of the family and the lineage; helped the dead to reach the other side; served as homage to their divinities; and protected the living and the dead. The shock effect of certain images could serve to ward off evil, and fulfilled a specific 'ritual' or psychological function in the context of religious and funerary art and space.

Finally, the emphasis on elite married couples, so clearly a crucial motif in Etruscan art, denoted the importance of the family in this aristocratic world. This Etruscan emphasis on couples, both divine and human, constitutes one of the chief differences between Greek and Etruscan attitudes, and accounts for the high position of women in Etruscan society, where the wife's family played as important a role in the family's genealogy as that of the husband. The aristocratic couple, in contrast to the world of the male citizen of the democratic Athenian society, or the *pater familias* of oligarchic Roman society, was the social basis of Etruscan life. Related to this emphasis on couples is the presence of children and family groups.

What happened to the Etruscans? Many died in the course of the wars of the second and first centuries BC. But by the time of the emperor Claudius the Etruscans had disappeared along with their language. Those who had survived the Civil Wars had become Romanised, and some achieved high office. Etruscan priests, with their books of prophecies, continued to be revered. But only the Etruscan name survived, as one of the regions of Roman Italy, Etruria.

FIG.49: *Sketch of Hades in a wolfskin cap inspired by an Etruscan tomb-painting, perhaps the example from the Tomb of Orcus on which the chapter heading of this book is based. Early sixteenth century, from the circle of Michelangelo.*

The Etruscan Pantheon

The following list gives information about Italic and Etruscan divinities, as well as Greek divinities who appear in Etruscan contexts. Many figures and their names are known from scenes represented on Etruscan gems, mirrors and other artefacts, and from votive inscriptions dedicating gifts to the gods.

Greek divinities sometimes retain only the name and a few of their connotations in Greek art and literature. This is the case for example with the Underworld demon Charu (Greek Charon, FIG.18), or the seer Chalchas (Greek Calchas, FIG.4). We know their Etruscan names from inscriptions which transcribe the Greek word into Etruscan.

The Etruscans, like the Romans after them, adopted many of the stories and characters of Greek mythology. There was some overlap, because they identified most of their own native divinities with those of the Greek pantheon. But, by and large, gods whom they worshipped in their religion were not the gods of mythology whom they represented in art. The gods named on the Piacenza Liver and the Zagreb linen wrappings are the gods to whom they prayed. Some of these were given the names of more or less similar Greek divinities. We know from inscriptions on mirrors, for example, that Nethuns on the Zagreb linen book was identified with Neptune. Hercle, Tinia, Uni and Fufluns, all of whose names appear on the Piacenza Liver, were identified respectively with Heracles, Zeus, Hera and Dionysos. There may also be other counterparts: some otherwise unknown names appearing on the Piacenza Liver may be epithets of known divinities.

Their native religion and their mythology, much of it imported, were more separate for the Etruscans than they were for the Greeks, though the Greeks, too, had gods who were more important in religion than in mythology, and vice versa. In many cases the Etruscan character of the god or goddess does not exactly coincide with that of the Greek deity. A number of divinities lack a stable iconography: Zeus/Tinia is sometimes shown as a youthful god, unlike his mature Greek counterpart, and minor divinities like Achvizr, Thalna and Lasa Sitmica can change gender, appearing as female or male figures.

Aita, Eita (Hades/Pluto/Dis). This elder god has a noble appearance, and wears a wolfskin cap (FIG. 49 and chapter heading image). He appears together with his wife Phersipnai (Persephone) ruling over the Underworld. The two are shown enthroned in tomb paintings in Tarquinia and on other monuments, including an incised mirror and a sarcophagus from Torre San Severo (Orvieto).

Apulu, Aplu (Apollo). Son of Letun (Leto) and brother of Aritimi (Artemis), the Greek god of prophecy, music and youth is known by his Greek name, transcribed into Etruscan. He

FIG.50: *Life-sized painted terracotta figure of Apollo. The image was originally placed on the ridgepole of the roof of a temple in the Portonaccio sanctuary at Veii, Rome, c. 510 BC.*

was an important god in Etruscan religion, where prophecy was essential in informing humans of the will of the gods. Apollo can be recognized by his good looks and attributes: the laurel bough and laurel crown, and the cithara or lyre which identifies him as the god of music, leader of the Muses. The bow and arrow show his destructive power; it is the opposite of his power to heal, as the god of medicine and father of Asklepios. He wears a necklace and bulla bracelet, like fashionable Etruscan youths, and appears on mirrors with his sister Artemis (Aritimi) or with a nymph. He is a spectator in important scenes such as the Adoption of Hercle by Uni (FIG. 20), and is shown in quiet conversation scenes together with other gods. Later Hellenistic funerary urns sometimes show his sanctuary at Delphi, characterized by a mound-like altar, the navel of the world. According to Greek myth Apollo was often in conflict with his brother Heracles, who stole the sacred tripod from the god's sanctuary at Delphi. The famous terracotta statue of the Veii Apollo, from the decoration of the temple at Veii (FIG. 50), shows the god striding forward. Facing him on the temple roof was Heracles, and between them the Kerynaean hind, over which they are fighting. It belonged to Artemis, and Heracles had been sent to bring it back as one of his Labours.

Achlae (Acheloos). In Greek mythology, he was the son of Okeanos and Tethys. Greek art shows him as a horned river god with the body of a bull, struggling with Heracles. Heracles breaks off his horn, which becomes the Cornucopia or Horn of Plenty. The conflict between Heracles and Acheloos ends with the death of Acheloos. His bearded head was often represented in Etruscan art and on lockets and jewellery as a good-luck charm. The image of this frontal male face with horns was evidently believed to frighten away evil spirits and to be a sign of good luck (FIG.40).

Aritimi, Artumes (Artemis/Diana). Apollo's twin sister, often appearing with him on mirrors. She is closely involved with her brother: a bronze statuette of the god bears a votive inscription dedicating it to his sister 'Aritimi'. Aritimi was worshipped in sanctuaries, where many votive offerings were made to her.

Athrpa (Atropos). According to Greek mythology, Atropos was one of the three Fates. On a mirror in Berlin she appears as a beautiful nude figure, hammering in place the inexorable nail of Fate in the presence of other divinities (FIG. 34).

Atunis (Adonis). The lover of Aphrodite. Both Greek and Etruscan art emphasized his youth. Etruscan art shows him in an amorous embrace with the goddess, sometimes as a very young boy. This is one of many cases of older goddesses shown with much younger lovers (FIG. 37).

Castur and Pultuce (Castor and Pollux). These Heavenly Twins, the sons of Zeus, appear more frequently on incised Etruscan mirrors than any other characters from Greek mythology. Since they were identical twins, their symmetry made them ideally suited for decorating mirrors. They were important in Etruscan religion, and were worshipped as divinities, as we know from votive gifts. On a votive inscription on the foot of a Greek vase, their names are translated into Etruscan as 'Tinas cliniar', the sons of Zeus. Castor and Pollux joined the Argonauts on the quest for the Golden Fleece, and appear with the others on an engraved fourth-century bronze *cista* or toilet box from Praeneste (Rome, Museo di Villa Giulia.

Catmite (Ganymede). In Greek mythology, Ganymede was a beautiful youth (FIG. 51). Zeus fell in love with him, and took the shape of an eagle to take him to Mount Olympos to be a cupbearer to the gods, where he became the male counterpart to Hebe. He appears in Greek and Etruscan art borne aloft by an eagle, soaring upward on outspread wings. His Etruscan name, Catmite, derives from Greek 'Gadymedes' (instead of Ganymedes), and the Latin name Catamitus comes from the Etruscan (the English word 'catamite').

Cel. One of a number of mother goddesses (ati Cel), perhaps Mother Earth, like the Greek Ge. The name appears on the Piacenza Liver. A votive inscription

FIG. 51: *A winged youth with swan's head cap, perhaps Catmite (Ganymede) pouring wine from a jug into a libation bowl. From a bronze lamp, north Etruscan, c. 300–200 BC.*

on five bronze statuettes reads *mi cels atial celthi*, 'I (belong) to Cel the mother, in the sanctuary of Cel.'

Celsclan. 'Son of Cel', a giant, and so son of Ge, Mother Earth. He appears on a mirror, with rays (of light?) issuing from his head, pursued by the armed Laran (Ares) in a scene from a battle of gods and giants.

Charun (Charon). The name appears to translate that of the Greek Charon, the boatman of the Underworld. Other than his location in the Underworld, however, there is little evidence of any connection of the Etruscan figure with the Greek boatman. Charu, whose attribute is the hammer, often appears together with his partner, Vanth, ready to guide the dead to the Underworld (FIG.18).

Culsans. The Etruscan Janus, keeper of the gate ('cul alp' on the Piacenza Liver), is a purely Etruscan divinity or demon. Culsu, the female equivalent of Culsans, is a demon dressed like Vanth, who appears on the sarcophagus of Hasti Afunei, from Chiusi. The cult of Culsu is recorded on the epitaph of Laris Pulenas (FIG.17).

Esplace (Asklepios/Aesculapius). According to Greek myth Asklepios, the god of healing, was the son of Apollo, who snatched him as an unborn child from the womb of his mother Koronis. Apollo gave him to the wise centaur Cheiron to raise and teach him the art of healing. Asklepios (Esplace) appears on an Etruscan mirror, bandaging the wounds of Prometheus (Prumathe) in the presence of Hercle and Menrva (FIG.23).

Fufluns (Dionysos/Bacchus). Fufluns, the Etruscan name for Dionysos, appears on the Piacenza Liver, so we know that he was important in Etruscan religion. The god of wine is also important in Etruscan mythology. He is shown in scenes like those which characterize him in Greek art – with his cortege of satyrs and maenads, or together with his bride

Ariadne. But he is also shown with his mother Semele (Semla), a couple not often illustrated in Greek art. Several curious scenes are unique to Etruscan art. One involves the story, told in the Greek 'Hymn to Dionysos', of his capture at sea by Tyrrhenian – that is, Etruscan(!) – pirates. Unaware of who he is, they plan to hold him for ransom. Dionysos reveals his identity and his power by transforming the pirates into dolphins, who then dive into the sea. An Etruscan vase now in Toledo illustrates this scene. Another scene shows the moment preceding his conception. Tinia, his father, holds his lightning bolt while he embraces his mother Semla: she lifts her skirt, uncovering her sexual parts and offering herself to him.

Hercle, Hercele, Herecele (Heracles/Hercules). In Etruscan mythology and religion Hercle was worshipped as a full-fledged god (FIGS 20, 21, 22). His name appears on the Piacenza Liver, and at his sanctuary at Cerveteri worshippers left votive gifts – statuettes and miniature clubs – inscribed with his name. Both Greek and Etruscan artists identify him in art by his standard attributes, the club and lion skin. Hercle is the most popular hero represented on gems, which were made for men in contrast to mirrors, which were made for women. His epithet is Calanice, 'beautifully victorious' (from the Greek 'Kallinikos'). His exploits are discussed on pages 34–39.

Laran (Ares/Mars). The warrior god is regularly shown armed, with helmet, shield and spear, in both Greek and Etruscan art. Etruscan craftsmen produced many votive figures of this god, a parallel to statuettes of the armed goddess Menerva (FIG.52). Laran also appears on a few mirrors, often armed and bearded, but sometimes as a nude youth with helmet, sword or spear. He is usually a spectator, but on one mirror he pursues

Celsclan in what looks like part of a battle of gods and giants.

Lasa. One of several nymphs associated with the circle of Turan, Lasa is usually represented on mirrors of the later Hellenistic period as a beautiful young woman, often winged and nude, holding a sash or an alabastron and perfume dipper. She appears by herself, or attending the embraces of divine couples. On one mirror Lasa is shown dressed and winged, holding a scroll with her own name and the names of doomed heroes, seemingly taking the place of Vanth (FIG.14). There is also a representation of a Lasa Sitmica who is a male figure. The name is found on the Piacenza Liver, as well as decorated mirrors and a gold ring.

Menerva, Menrva (Athena/Minerva). The goddess's Latin name, Minerva, comes from the Etruscan. She is one of the principal Etruscan and Italic divinities, and her name appears on numerous monuments, though not on the Piacenza Liver. Etruscan artists showed her dressed in the Greek manner in a peplos with overfold, and armed with helmet, shield and spear. They also represented her birth from the head of her father (FIG.28), and her participation in the Judgement of Paris along with the two other goddesses, Hera (Uni) and Aphrodite (Turan) (FIG.1). Like the Greek Athena, she protects heroes like Perseus (FIG.31) and Heracles. Sometimes, as on the Boccanera plaques (FIG.1), only the spear identifies her. Her character is different from that of the Greek goddess of war, strategy and wisdom. In Italy some of her multiple functions include attending scenes of love, healing and birth, confronting a monster, and even appearing on one mirror in the role of a *kourotrophos* or baby-sitter, looking after a group of babies.

Nethuns (Poseidon/Neptune). He was the Italic, Umbrian god of springs and water, and an important divinity in

FIG.52: *Bronze figures of Athena and Ares (Menerva and Laran) made in Umbria under Etruscan influence. Such elongated figures are believed to have inspired the artist Alberto Giacometti. Fifth century* BC.

Etruscan religion. He differs from the Greek Poseidon, though he often bears the trident which identifies him as god of the sea. On one mirror, he appears with Usil, the sun god, and Thesan, the Dawn (Eos, Aurora). His name appears frequently on the Zagreb mummy bandages as a deity to whom offerings of wine are to be made, and twice on the Piacenza Liver.

Phersipnai, Phersipnei (Persephone/ Proserpina). Daughter of Demeter, known as Kore in Greek mythology. In Etruscan art she appears most frequently together with her husband, Aita (Hades), as part of the divine couple, rulers of the Underworld. She is labelled

'Prosepnai' on a mirror, a name related to the Latin Proserpina.

Sethlans (Hephaistos/Vulcan). In spite of his Etruscan name, the god corresponds closely to the character of the Greek and Roman god of fire, the forge and craftsmen in general, Hephaistos. Like Hephaistos, his attributes are the hammer, tongs and axe, and the *pileus* or workman's cap. On Etruscan mirrors Sethlans appears as the divine craftsman. On one occasion, he is about to split Tinia's head open to facilitate the birth of Menrva. Another time he frees Uni from a throne in which he had imprisoned her. An assistant named Tretu helps. On another occasion he makes the Trojan Horse (which here is apparently bronze and named Pecse or Pegasus) with the help of an assistant named Etule (FIG.27). Appropriately, his head appears on coins of Populonia, a city famed for its flourishing metallurgical industry.

Thesan (Eos/Aurora). The goddess of Morning and Dawn, or Aurora, appears driving her chariot, as in Greek art, with her son Memnun (Memnon) who was killed by Achilles (Achle), or carrying off one of her young lovers, Tithonus or Kephalos. Thesan was worshipped in Etruscan religion: her name appears on the Zagreb mummy wrappings and on a bronze tablet from Pyrgi.

Tinia, Tina, Tin (Zeus/Jove/Jupiter). God of daylight and chief of the gods, he was identified with the Greek and Roman king of gods and men. In art he holds the thunderbolt, his most consistent attribute, usually shown like two stylized flower buds joined back to back. The thunderbolt is the sign of his power: according to the sacred books of the Etruscans, thunderbolts, when properly interpreted, revealed to mankind the will of the gods. Tinia is usually represented according to the classical Greek iconography of Zeus enthroned in majesty, epitomized by

Pheidias's cult statue of Zeus at Olympia (FIG.28). The imposing bearded figure sits partially draped (a guise conventionally known as heroic semi-nudity) and wearing a crown often of oak leaves rather than the olive wreath of Greek depictions. He is also sometimes shown as a youthful, unbearded male. In Etruscan religion the god was worshipped either alone, in the company of his wife, Uni (FRONTISPIECE) or as the central figure of the so-called Capitoline triad. This group of three divinities, which appears in Roman art, consisted of Tinia, Uni (Hera, Juno) and Menrva (Athena). The group is named after the statues of the three gods which stood together in the tripartite cella of the Etruscan temple of Jupiter Optimus Maximus, 'Best and Greatest.' The temple, on the Capitoline Hill in Rome, was commissioned by the Tarquins, the Etruscan kings of Rome, and decorated by the Etruscan artist Vulca of Veii.

Tiur (Selene/Luna). Goddess of the moon. Her name appears on the Piacenza Liver, next to Usil, and on a large bronze votive offering shaped like a crescent moon.

Tuchulcha. A bestial, terrifying demon of death, with vulture's beak, donkey's ears and writhing snakes. This terrible demon appears by the seated These (Theseus) in the Underworld in the Tomb of Orcus II in Tarquinia. His head, like Charun's, has a hooked nose and wild hair, and his flesh is the bluish colour of rotting meat. His image inspired the demon in Michelangelo's Last Judgement (FIG.44).

Turan (Aphrodite/Venus). She is the goddess of love and passion, one of the most important Etruscan divinities, and appears often on Etruscan monuments, especially mirrors. In the early period, and often later too, she is richly dressed, but in the Hellenistic period her most consistent characteristic is her nudity. She appears in toilette scenes (FIG.2), in the Judgement of Paris together with

Uni and Menrva (FIG.1), or with her young lover, Adonis (Atunis) (FIG.25). She has an entourage composed of Eros/Cupid, her attendants and her swan, Tusna ('swan of Turan'). She helps her protégés by inspiring women to fall in love with them, for example Medea, whom she fills with passion to help Jason bring back the Golden Fleece; and Helen, whom she persuades to run away with Paris. Turan was worshipped at the Greek sanctuary of Gravisca, the harbour of Tarquinia, and elsewhere, as shown by votive offerings inscribed with her name. Once she is called 'Turan ati' or Mother Turan, perhaps connecting her with the Roman Venus Genetrix, mother of Aeneas and his descendants, the Julian line.

Turms (Hermes/Mercury). The Greek Hermes, the messenger god is shown equipped with winged sandals, travelling hat and herald's staff. The Etruscan Turms has the same attributes and the same functions as in Greek religion. He accompanies gods and heroes on their missions, conducts the goddesses to the Judgement of Paris (FIG.1) or delivers the egg of Helen to her parents, Latva and Tuntle (Leda and Tyndareus) (FIG.3). An important duty is to escort the dead on the dangerous journey to the Underworld. On a mirror from Vulci he conducts the shade of Teiresias ('hinthial terasias') to Uthuze (Odysseus) (FIG.19). His epithet, 'turms aitas', (Hermes of Hades), is the equivalent of the Greek, Hermes Psychopompos, 'who leads souls [to Hades]'.

Uni (Hera/Juno). The name of the Roman queen of the gods, Iuno (Juno), is related to that of the Etruscan Uni; the name has the -i ending of the feminine gender in the Etruscan language. Her name may mean 'the goddess of youth', *iuvenis*. According to Greek myth she is the sister and wife of Zeus, jealous of his many love affairs and particularly resentful of Heracles.

The Etruscan Uni is more important in Etruscan art and religion than her counterpart in the Greek pantheon, and her relationship with both Tinia or Zeus and his son Heracles is quite different (FIG.20). Husband and wife are shown together as a devoted couple (FRONTISPIECE). She is often enthroned, like her husband, and she wears a diadem and other jewellery. Uni appears in scenes of the Judgement of Paris together with Turan and Menrva, or preparing for the contest (FIG.1). On the bilingual Pyrgi tablets she is identified with the Near Eastern and Phoenician goddess Astarte, or Ishtar, who is elsewhere seen as a counterpart of the Greek Aphrodite, the goddess of love.

Usil (Helios/Sol). God of the sun. His name appears on the Piacenza Liver, next to Tiur, the moon. On two mirrors he appears with a halo, on one with Nethuns, god of the sea, and Thesan, goddess of the dawn, and on the other with Uprium (Hyperion).

FIG.53: *Winged, striding figure of Vanth with bearded snakes entwined around her arms. Found near Mount Vesuvius. Bronze, c. 425–400 BC.*

Vanth. This winged, female demon of death accompanies the deceased to the Underworld, brandishing torches, bearded snakes or scrolls. She appears in Etruscan art of the fourth and third centuries nude, semi-nude, or dressed like Artemis the huntress or a Fury on south Italian vases, with short *chiton* (tunic), high boots and straps crossed between naked breasts. She is one of the most impressive figures in the Etruscan pantheon. A bronze statuette shows her striding purposefully, grasping bearded snakes wound around her arms (FIG.53). She wears a Greek *peplos* with overfold, and her feet barely touch the ground as she moves rapidly forward like an angel of death. Vanth often appears together with Charu[n], as in the Tomb of the Anina (FIG.18) or the sarcophagus of Laris Pulenas (FIG.17). The two are often added to scenes of Greek mythology. In the François Tomb, Vanth's rainbow-coloured wings are outspread behind Achilles and Patroclus (Achle and Patrucle). On a vase painting from Orvieto she is dancing, naked, and looks like a Maenad, but holds a scroll on which her name, Vanth, is recorded. She is present at but not involved in death, and is sometimes given the role of a Greek Fury.

Etruscan name	Greek equivalent	Roman equivalent
Aita, Eita	Hades	Pluto, Dis
Apulu, Aplu	Apollo	Apollo
Achlae	Acheloos	
Aritimi, Artumes	Artemis	Diana
Athrpa (one of the Fates)	Atropos	Atropos
Atunis	Adonis	Adonis
Tinas cliniar (sons of Zeus)	Dioskouroi	Dioscuri
Castur, Pultuce	Kastor, Polydeukes	Castor, Pollux
Catmite	Ganymede	Ganymede
Charun, Charu	Charon	Charon
Culsans		Janus
Esplace	Asklepios	Asclepius
Fufluns	Dionysos	Bacchus
Hercle, Hercele, Herecele	Heracles	Hercules
Laran	Ares	Mars
Menarva, Menrva	Athena	Minerva
Nethuns	Poseidon	Neptune
Phersipnai, Phersipnei	Persephone	Proserpina
Sethlans	Hephaistos	Vulcan
Tinia, Tina, Tin	Zeus	Jove, Jupiter
Thesan (goddess of the dawn)	Eos	Aurora
Tiur (the moon goddess)	Selene	Luna
Turan	Aphrodite	Venus
Turms	Hermes	Mercury
Uni	Hera	Juno
Usil	Helios	Sol

Suggestions for Further Reading

Larissa Bonfante (ed.), *Etruscan Life and Afterlife: a handbook of Etruscan studies* (Detroit, 1986)

Larissa Bonfante, 'Etruscan' in *'Reading the Past. Ancient Writing from Cuneiform to the Alphabet* (London, 1990)

Giuliano Bonfante and Larissa Bonfante, *The Etruscan Language: an Introduction*, 2nd edn (Manchester, 2002)

Federica Borelli and Maria Cristina Targia, *The Etruscans: art, architecture, and history* (London, 2004)

Otto Brendel, *Etruscan Art* (New Haven and London, 1995)

Lucilla Burn, *Greek Myths* (London and Austin, 1990)

Thomas H. Carpenter, *Art and Myth in Ancient Greece: a handbook* (London, 1991)

Timothy Gantz, *Early Greek Myth. A Guide to Literary and Artistic Sources* (Baltimore and London, 1996)

Nancy de Grummond and Erika Simon (eds.), *The Religion of the Etruscans* (Austin, 2005)

Nancy de Grummond, *Etruscan Myth* (Philadelphia, 2006)

Sybille Haynes, *Etruscan Civilisation: a cultural history* (London, 2000)

Tom Rasmussen and Graeme Barker, *The Etruscans* (Oxford, 1998)

Nigel Spivey, *Etruscan Art* (London, 1997)

Stephan Steingräber, *Etruscan Painting* (Los Angeles, 2006)

Mario Torelli (ed.) *The Etruscans* (Venice, 2000)

L.B. van der Meer, *Interpretatio Etrusca: Greek myths on Etruscan mirrors* (Amsterdam, 1995)

Susan Woodford, *Images of Myths in Classical Antiquity* (Cambridge, 2003)

LIMC (Lexicon Iconographicum Mythologiae Classicae). Illustrated encyclopaedia of characters from Greek, Roman and Etruscan mythology in eight double volumes, over 30,000 photographs, two volumes of indices. Compiled by an international team of scholars.

Corpus Speculorum Etruscorum (CSE) International catalogue of all Etruscan mirrors in public and private collections around the world, fully illustrated. Organized by the Istituto di Studi Etruschi, Florence.

Picture credits
Many of the drawings of mirrors in this book are from the *Corpus Speculorum Etruscorum* series (CSE). Figures 4, 19, 20, 27, 34 and 37 are from *Etruskische Spiegel* (vols I-V, 1843-1897). Figures 16 and 45 are from *Monumenti Inediti* (Rome, vols VIII-IX, 1864-1873).

Archivio Buonarotti, Florence: 49; Bibliothèque Nationale, Cabinet des Médailles, Paris: 29 (courtesy of Dr.I.Aghion); The British Museum, London: cover: GR: 1889.4-10.3; frontispiece: GR 1824.4-53.11; 1: GR 1889.4-10.1,4,2; 21: GR1824.4-46.22; 25: GR1847.11-1.21; 26: GR 1772.3-15.366; 32: CM 1937.6-6.30; 40: GR 1884.6-14.16; 42: GR 1859.8-16.1, 47: GR 1877.8-2.1; 52: GR 1824.4-54.25; 53: GR 1824.4-13.3, 1814.7-4.962; 54: GR 1864.3-16.1; Drawings by Susan Bird (from CSE Great Britain 1,1): 2: GR 1865.1-3.39; 8: GR 1865.7-12.4,9; GR 1847.9-9.2; 14: GR 1847.9-9.4; 15: GR 1900.6-11.3; 22: GR1772.3-4.74; 28: GR 1873.8-20.105; 31: GR 1888.11-10.1; 35: GR 1922.4-13.27; 38: GR 1873.8-20.105. Drawings by Kate Morton: map; 41; chapter heading image; Deutsche Archeologische Institut, Berlin: 18 (courtesy of Dr S. Steingräber); Dr E. F. Macnamara: 13; Kunsthistorisches Museum, Vienna: 36 (courtesy of Dr.K.Zhuber-Okrog and T.Ritter); The Metropolitan Museum of Art, New York: 5 (drawn and reproduced by kind permission of Dr A. Emiliozzi), 23, 30 and 33 (drawings by E. Wahle, from CSE USA 3, 1997); Musée du Louvre, Paris: 45 © Photo RMN, © René-Gabriel Ojéda; Museo Archeologico Nazionale, Florence: 3 (courtesy of Dr G.C.Cianferoni and Dr M.C.Guidotti, Soprintendenza per i Beni Archeologici di Firenze); Museum of Fine Art, Boston: 7 (drawing by R. De Puma, from CSE USA 2,1993); The National Maritime Museum, London: 48; Scala Archives: 6 © 1990, Museo Nazionale, Tarquinia, Soprintendenza per I Beni Archeologici di Firenze; 10 Museo Etrusco di Villa Giulia; 51 © 2004 (courtesy of the Ministero per I Beni e le Attività Culturali); 11 © 1990, Museo Guarnacci, Volterra; 12 © 2003, Museo Guarnacci, Volterra; 17 © 2005, Museo Nazionale, Tarquinia; 39 © 1990, Musei Capitolini, Rome; 43 © 2000; 44 © 1999. All images © Photo Scala.

Index

Acheron, Achrum 10
Achilles 14, 15, 16, 17, 18, 19, 20, 29, 45, 55, 56, 57, 58, 76, 78
Acheloos 53, 54, 72
Achvizr 14, 50, 71
Actaeon 58
Admetus 47
Adonis 48, 49, 51, 73, 77
Aigisthos 20
Aeneas 11, 59, 60, 64, 77
Aeschylus 22, 26
Agamemnon 14, 15, 20, 29, 33, 56, 67, 68
Ajax 18, 19, 20, 26, 27, 29, 57
Alkmene 34, 36
Amazons 37, 58
Amphiaraos 19, 26, 27, 47, 60
Amphitryon 34
Andromache 20
Andromeda 44
Anina family 31, 33, 67, 78
Annunciation 66
Antigone 22, 27
Aphrodite 11, 12, 13, 14, 15, 20, 48, 49, 50, 51, 59, 60, 73, 75, 76, 77
Apollo 10, 18, 21, 35, 37, 41, 51, 52, 72, 73
Ara Maxima 61
Ara Pacis 64
Ares 59, 74, 75
Argonauts 73
Argos 20, 36
Ariadne 40, 41, 51, 52, 74
Artemis 10, 15, 37, 47, 51, 55, 56, 57, 58, 59, 72, 73, 78
Artile 52, 53, 60
Asklepios 38, 39, 72, 74
Astarte 9, 10, 49
Astyanax 20
Atalanta 46, 47, 48
Athena 10, 11, 12, 14, 19, 20, 23, 34, 36, 38, 39, 42, 43, 44, 45, 46, 50, 55, 57, 59, 75, 76
Atlas 39
Atropos 48, 52, 60, 73
Augustus 59, 64, 65

Baubo 65
Bellerophon 42, 45, 46, 47
Boccanera plaques 12, 13, 75
Busiris, King of Egypt 39

Cacu 52, 61
Cacus 60, 61
Calchas 15, 52 71
Caligula 66
Calydonian Boar 46, 48
Calypso 28
Capaneus 24, 26
Capitoline Hill/Temple 59, 74
Capitoline Wolf 54, 65, 66, 68
Cassandra 20, 55, 56
Castor 14, 15, 47, 73
Catha 10
Cel, Celsclan 10, 73, 74, 75
Cerberus 37
Chalchas 15, 16, 52, 60, 71
Charon 29, 71, 74
Charu[n] 31, 33, 51, 55, 56,

57, 66, 67, 71, 74, 76, 77, 78
Chimaera 42, 46, 47, 65
Cicero 58
Circe 28, 29
Claudius 64, 70
Cloelia 62
Clytemnestra 14, 20, 56
Culsans 74
Culsu 74
Cyclops 29, 30, 60

Daidalos 40, 41, 42
Danae 42
Dante (Inferno) 24, 66, 67, 69
Deianeira 39
Demeter 65, 75
Dionysos 10, 41, 50, 51, 54, 71, 74
Dionysius of Halicarnassus 59

Eos 75, 76
Eros 49, 77
Eteocles 22, 26, 58
Euripides 19
Eurystheus 36
Evil Eye 53

fasces 68
Fate/s 14, 47, 48, 52, 60, 73
François Vase/Tomb 11, 20, 32, 57
Fury/Furies 56, 57, 78

Ganymede 73
Gauls 57, 58
Ge 73, 74
Geryon 30, 36, 60
giants 58, 74, 75
Giotto 66
Gorgon 17, 42, 44, 45, 53
Graiai 44, 45

Hades 28, 30, 33, 38, 44, 51, 53, 65, 72
Hannibal 58
Hebe 39, 73
Hebrews 58
Hektor 16, 20
Helen 12, 13, 14, 15, 20, 50, 55, 65, 77
Helios 77
Hephaistos 16, 59, 76
Hera 10, 11, 12, 13, 14, 21, 29, 33, 34, 35, 36, 49, 59, 71, 75, 76, 77
Heracles 19, 30, 34, 35, 36, 38, 39, 40, 49, 71, 72, 74, 75, 76, 77
Hermes 11, 12, 14, 15, 32, 33, 44, 46, 77
Hermione 15, 50
Hesperides 37, 38, 39
hinthial (ghost) 32, 50, 67, 68, 77
Homer 11, 15, 17, 28, 29, 30, 33, 56, 59, 60
Horatius Cocles 63
Hydra 36

Icarus 42
Iliad 11, 15, 16, 56, 60
Iliupersis 19, 28
Iolaos 36
Iphigeneia 15, 55, 56
Iphikles 34
Isaac 58

Ixion 29

Jason 47, 77

Labyrinth 40, 41, 42
Laris Pulenas 30, 33, 74, 78
Lasa/s 10, 26, 27, 50, 60, 71, 75
Leda 14, 15, 77
Leto 72
Livy 8, 58, 59, 60, 61, 62, 64
Lucretia 61, 64
Lucumo 61, 64

Macaulay, Thomas 62, 64
Mars 59, 60, 74
Mastarna 64
Medea 77
Medusa 44, 45, 46, 47, 53
Melanippos 23, 26, 58, 66
Meleager 47, 48
Memnon 76
Menelaos 14, 15, 20, 54
Mezentius 58, 60, 64
Michelangelo 66, 67, 68, 70, 76
Minos 40, 42
Minotaur 40, 41, 42, 44, 50
Mlacuch 37
Monteleone Chariot 16, 17, 45
Mucius Scaevola 62, 64

Nathum 56
Nekyuia 28
Nemean Lion 36
Nemesis 14, 15
Neoptolemus, son of Achilles 20
Nessos, centaur 39
Nestor 47
Numa Pompilius 59
Nymphs 44, 49, 51, 75

Odysseus 19, 28, 29, 30, 32, 33, 77
Oedipus 20, 21, 22, 23, 58
Orestes/Oresteia 56
Orcus 29, 30, 32, 33, 67, 68, 70, 76

Paris 11, 12, 13, 14, 15, 50, 55, 75, 76, 77, 78
Pasiphae 40, 42, 44, 50
Patroclus 16, 56, 57, 78
Pausanias 28
Pegasus 45, 46, 47, 76
Peleus 11, 14, 47
Penelope 28
Persephone 30, 38, 51, 65, 72, 75
Perseus 36, 42, 44, 45, 46, 74
Phaedra 40
Phoenician 9, 40, 49, 77
Piacenza Liver 10, 15, 71, 74, 75, 76, 77
Pirithoos 30, 38, 47
Pliny 65, 69
Plutarch 59
Pollaiuolo, Antonio 65
Pollux 14, 15, 47, 73
Polygnotos 28
Polyneices 22, 26, 27, 58
Polyphemos 30
Polyxena 20, 55
Porsenna, Lars 62, 63, 64

Poseidon 45, 59, 75
Priam 14, 16, 17, 20,
Prometheus 38, 39, 74
Priapus 65

Rhea Silvia 64
Roma, goddess 65
Romulus 11, 53, 54, 59, 60, 64, 65
Remus 53, 54, 60, 65

satyr/s 13, 41, 50, 51, 54, 74
Selene 76, 77, 78
Semele 41, 51, 52, 74
Servius Tullius see Mastarna
Shakespeare 64
Signorelli, Luca 66
Sirens 28
Sisyphos 29, 30, 31, 32, 33
Sophocles 21
Sphinx/sphinxes 12, 21, 22, 53, 65
Styx 29

Tanaquil 61, 64
Tantalos 29
Tarquins 53, 59, 61, 62, 64, 76
Teiresias 28, 29, 32, 33, 50, 68, 77
Telemachos 28
Terra Mater 65
Thalna 50, 71
Thebes 21, 22, 23, 24, 26, 27, 34, 58
Theopompus 52
Theseus 30, 38, 40, 41, 47, 76
Thetis 11, 14, 16, 17, 20
Troilos 17, 18, 55, 58
Trojan Horse 19, 20, 42, 43, 76
Trojan War 11–20, 27, 28, 55
Troy 14, 15, 16, 19, 20, 28, 56
Tuchulcha 30, 66, 77
Tullia 61
Tusna, swan of Turan 49, 51, 77
Tydeus 23, 26, 58, 66
Tyndareus 14, 15, 77

Underworld 28, 29, 30, 31, 33, 34, 37, 38, 41, 51, 53, 55, 65, 67, 68, 70, 72, 74, 75, 76, 77, 78

Vanth 26, 27, 30, 31, 33, 51, 55, 56, 57, 66, 74, 75, 77, 78
Venus 59, 60, 65, 76, 77
Vestal Virgin 60
Victory 69
Vipinas, Caile and Avile (Vibenna brothers, Aulus and Caelus) 53, 60
Virgil 58, 59, 60
Vulca 76

Zagreb 10, 71, 75, 76
Zeus 10, 11, 14, 20, 24, 27, 29, 31, 32, 33, 34, 35, 36, 38, 40, 42, 43, 49, 50, 52, 59, 71, 73, 74, 76, 77, 78
Zipna 51